An "Extra Special Message" to you from Robert A. Schuller

Dear "Partner in Possibilities:"

As I celebrate, with my father, our 30 years of ministry and 15 years of Hour of Power on TV, we wish to extend to you an "extra special thank you" for the special effort you have made in making the Robert Schuller Ministry everything that it is on this, our 30th Anniversary.

As we look to the future, thank you for keeping this ministry alive and giving us the hope that together we can look forward to another 15, 30 or 40 years with excitement and anticipation — for you have made it possible.

It is my prayer that as you read the stories contained in this book you will be uplifted and motivated by the extraordinary people who have succeeded in the ordinary world.

It is my hope that you will be motivated and inspired to become an extraordinary person in your own right, so that as you continue to live for Christ His love will continue to shine in your life giving you an "extra special" spiritual source for ministry — Jesus Christ.

Our future for our continued ministry is exciting, thanks to you, and your support of the Hour of Power ministry.

God loves you and so do I!

Robert A. Schuller

Robert Schuller Ministries
Celebrating 30 years in ministry
1955–1985
Hour of Power
Celebrating 15 years on TV
1970–1985

ROBERT H. SCHULLER

TELLS YOU HOW TO ...

BE AN EXTRAORDINARY PERSON IN AN ORDINARY WORLD

Edited By
ROBERT A. SCHULLER

Fleming H. Revell Company
Old Tappan, New Jersey

Scripture quotations are the author's paraphrase.

Library of Congress Cataloging in Publication Data
Schuller, Robert Harold.
    Robert H. Schuller tells you how to be an extraordinary
person in an ordinary world.

    Includes index.
    1. Christian life—Reformed authors.   2. Success.
    3. Schuller, Robert Harold.   I. Schuller, Robert A.
II. Title
BV4501.2.S322   1985   248.4′85732   84-27539
ISBN 0-8007-1419-9

*It is an honor for me to be able to dedicate this book
to the most extraordinary person I know:
my wife, Donna Michelle Schuller.
Without her this book would not exist.*

Contents

CONTENTS

CONTENTS

Introduction by
Robert A. Schuller

What has the charm or the power of a story? For a child, the world is created anew every time he hears those magic words, "Once upon a time. . . ." And adults? How many of us live vicariously, even model ourselves and our attitudes on "Dallas" or "Dynasty" or the personal stories on the "Hour of Power"? Stories aren't neutral. In a very real sense the stories we choose become the stories we live.

I was a privileged child: there were good stories in our house, stories of adventure and excitement. Some of my fondest memories are of my father holding me in his lap just before bedtime while he read the Bible to me and my sisters or told us stories about people he knew—real people who overcame great odds, did good works, or just took the little gray corner of their world and painted it with the glorious color of love for all the people around them.

My father's stories did more than excite us. They motivated us at a deep and profound level. They showed us that there is no ordinary world if you have the grace to see that God is in it. And there are no ordinary people . . . each and every one of us is extraordinary because God made us. (And, as that child says in a wonderful little story my father often tells, "God don't make no junk!")

Robert H. Schuller is an extraordinary man. Not because he's the pastor of the Crystal Cathedral, or the author of best-selling books, or seen nationally on the "Hour of Power." He's extraordinary because he's grasped this simple truth: Jesus Christ taught in stories and parables . . . and He must have had a good reason. Stories stick with you. They stuck with me. What I have learned of love, generosity, honesty, and the love of God I learned from my father, and the stories he told. The life he lives exemplifies those stories.

The people you will meet in this book are life changers. They are heroic men and women who took their defeats, infirmities, disasters, and depressions and turned them into works for the Lord. They changed their lives for the better, and their stories will change your life if you allow yourself to believe and adopt their powerful remedies for "ordinary human existence."

Here they are as my father has captured their extraordinary character and spirit in story:

Let Penny Cotton show you how to overcome illness.

Learn from Katherine Grant's unique ministry.

Live the experience of Allen Phillips, whose life was spared through his faith.

Love the world around you like Sara and Norm Rasmussen and watch it respond, grow, and be transformed.

Let these people show you that you too can Be an Extraordinary Person in an Ordinary World.

EXTRAORDINARY EXAMPLE

How to Handle Your Foes: Keep On Shining!

A judge was campaigning for reelection. He had a reputation for integrity. He was a distinguished and honorable gentleman of no small charity. His opponent was conducting a vicious, mud-smearing, unfair campaign against him.

Somebody approached the judge and asked, "Do you know what your opponent is saying about you? Do you know he is criticizing you? How are you going to handle it? What are you going to do about it?" The judge looked at his counselors and his campaign committee and calmly replied, "Well, when I was a boy I had a dog. And every time the moon was full, that hound dog would howl and bark at the bright face of the moon. We never did sleep very well those nights. He would bark and howl at the moon all night." With that, the judge concluded his remarks.

"That's beside the point," his campaign manager impatiently said. "You've told us a nice story about your dog, but what are you going to do about your critic?"

The judge explained, "I just answered you! When the dog barked at the moon, the moon kept right on shining! I don't intend to do anything but keep right on shining. And I'll ignore the criticism, as the moon ignored the dog. I'll just keep right on shining! Quietly, calmly, beautifully!"

Remember that! It might give you courage to sail—to strive for the top and not worry about what people say whether you succeed or you fail.

Called to Greatness

Recently I was in the Hawaiian Islands. I stopped at the Punch Bowl and looked at those acres and acres of little white crosses where the best and the bravest were buried. And I thought of this: Why did they step forward? Why did they say yes? Why did so many of them volunteer? Why did they not resist the draft? Why did they put the uniform on and wear it proudly? Why wasn't there a mass protest against the war? Why didn't we just say, "We're our own country here. Nobody's burning people in ovens in America. And sure, they dropped a bomb on Pearl Harbor, but that's three thousand miles away. Just let them have the island." Nobody said that. Why not? Why did the Americans rise up? What motivated them? What spark was ignited within them?

I think I know part of that answer. I was born and raised in Iowa and every Sunday morning we went to the little country church. And what I'm about to tell you is indicative of the social structure of the United States in the '20s, '30s, and '40s.

At that time everyone regularly attended church. And in the two hundred to three hundred thousand little churches all over the United States, fathers and mothers went to church and dedicated their children to the Lord. In that dedication the parents would pray that God would take the little child and make him do something beautiful for God, become a Christian, and maybe even go into the Lord's service. The greatest honor that could come to a father and mother would be if their child grew up and said, "Dad, I want to be a missionary. I want to become a doctor and build a hospital in Japan or Arabia or India."

18

Let me tell you, in the '20s, the '30s, and the '40s our heroes were called missionaries. And when they finally got through college, seminary, and medical school, they packed their bags and set off for the remote parts of the world before there was penicillin. The odds were that they might die of a tropical disease. They knew that.

Why did they go? They had a call—a call to greatness. It was the same for the many men who went to battle in World War II. They had a call to greatness. And after being at the Punch Bowl I have a message for all people: Do not pity the person who was killed in war. Rather, pity the person who's alive but doesn't have anything he'd die for, for the person who's never had a call to greatness. Greatness starts when you become aware of your mortality, when suddenly it dawns on you that you're going to die. You don't know when, and you don't know how, but the fact is—you're not immortal. With that consciousness comes a thought like this: *I want to make a mark—somehow, someway, somewhere."* Greatness comes when you are consumed by a call to make a commitment that may mean your very life.

No person is truly alive or totally human until he makes a commitment to something that he will gladly die for. That is a chariot of fire. It lifts you above the earth. It transcends the flesh and brings you into the realm of the spirit. Don't feel sorry for those who are buried under white crosses. Feel sorry for those who are alive and have nothing today that they would gladly die for.

A Very Bad Impression

A bus driver in Chicago had a female passenger who was really irritated by something. She let loose with a string of unrepeatable words. Everybody was ashamed. And then the bus stopped, the profane passenger got ready to disembark, and the bus driver said, "Madam, you left something behind." She asked him what it was and he said, "A very bad impression."

One Day in Seven

One day in seven. Now let's take this commandment. The Sabbath day. The Moslems set a day aside. It's Friday. The Jewish people set a day aside. It is Saturday. Most Christians set a day aside. It is the first day of the week, to commemorate the Resurrection of Jesus Christ. You need one day in seven. It is not an ordinary day if you know how to use it. I'll share with you how to use it, because Americans have given it up for the most part.

Traditionally, Sunday was a very great creative day of quietness for faith, for fun, for the family, for the church, and for the community. Something happened—and I make this statement here and now based on research that I have done—and that is, in the past fifty years we have seen a growing, deepening sense of depression in the widespread epidemic of emotional ailments such as anxiety and stress, with its effect upon the human organism. This emotional epidemic of negative, mental, and spiritual problems in our country has risen sharply in proportion to our forsaking of that one 'day in seven as a useful day for healing.

How can you use it? It's not an ordinary day if you know how to use it. Use it as a day of *rest*. You need one day in seven to rest the heart, the system, and the body. The Bible says, "In quietness and confidence shall be your strength" (*see* Isaiah 30:15). I try to work hard but I take Mondays off. My Sabbath, as you might expect, is not Sunday, and it's not the Jewish Saturday, and it's not the Moslem Friday. My Sabbath is Monday. I do not go into my office on that day, because if I can't get my work done in six days, I'm disorganized. Simple. And I would rather live longer and do more than try to accomplish a lot in a few years and die too young. We need one day. Use it for rest. And then use it for a day of retreat. Retreat from the tension-producing inputs that you have to be exposed to the rest of the week.

I'm eternally, profoundly indebted to Richard Neutra for the doctrine of biorealism. I never learned it in theology. But it's embedded in psychology and profound theology. His doctrine of biorealism is that the human being is created with a built-in tranquilizing system, with eyes to see the trees and the hills and colors of the flowers; ears to hear the singing of the birds and listen to the rustle of the leaves and the whisper of the wind; the nose to smell the fragrance of the flowers and the new-mown grass; the skin to feel the caress of the sun and cool breezes. It's a biological reality, and the biological reality is that God created this in order for these to be channels of tranquillity entering your system.

And so when God created Adam, he put him in a beautiful lush, green garden filled with the exotic fragrance of wild flowers and the melody of singing birds, not in an ugly parking lot where his senses would be assaulted by the wailing of sirens and the exhaust fumes from cars and

21

buses. And that's why when you are in the mountains, you feel the closeness with God. Of course, the bird was designed to fly, the fish was meant to swim, and you were designed to live in a garden. You were not designed to live in a concrete jungle.

So Richard Neutra said, "What can we do? We can't demolish our cities and bulldoze all the asphalt. We need the cars and we need the buses. What can we do? We have to design for emotional survival." You bet! So we design places where you can hear the birds sing, where you can look out and see the clouds drifting through the sky. And we try to create a garden retreat from the tension-producing sounds and sights of the world. That's why we need one day in seven. Now many of you live in cities. You don't live in a house. You don't live in a place where you're protected from those sights, so what do you do? I've got news for you. You go to church on Sunday. That's right! And that's why many churches are designed with stained-glass windows and solid walls. Because without them you'd look out on a parking lot with electric power poles. But in those beautiful retreat places called churches, the sounds and sights that would fill you with negative emotional tensions are released and the stress goes.

So it is in our family. Let me say something: We have a great family—I mean my wife and me and our five children. We have always kept Sunday as a day to rest; as a day to retreat—to retreat from the normal pressures of the week. I remember when our oldest daughter, Sheila, was about four years old, and her neighborhood playmate came to the house one Sunday asking if Sheila could come out and play. I wasn't prepared for that, and I said, "No, not today, but she can play tomorrow and the next day and every day the rest of the week, but not on Sunday." I wanted that one day completely different so that she was exposed to just the family and friends in the church—retreat. Let it be a day of rest. Let it be a day of retreat. Let it be a day to regroup. I mean regroup your thinking and get your act together.

The Introduction

I was in New Orleans to participate in the City Prayer Breakfast. It was a great, big, exciting event. The mayor of New Orleans was there along with twelve hundred other people. I had the honor of delivering the prayer-breakfast talk. Only minutes before I was to speak I got word that Jesse Jackson had decided to attend. He had flown in from Los Angeles, and would be arriving any minute. Suddenly, I saw him enter. When he made his entrance, everybody knew he was in the room.

Although I have been friends with Jesse for many years, his presence created a problem for me. I had been carefully briefed on protocol as to whom I should recognize by name before I started my speech. I had the introductions of the mayor, the senators, and the archbishops, all written out. But I did not have an introduction for Jesse Jackson. How could I recognize Jesse without appearing to personally endorse his candidacy?

When it was time for me to speak, I made a little announcement. I said, "Does anybody have a copy of the book *Tough Times Never Last, But Tough People Do?* Surely, someone came here this morning carrying a copy of that book. Would you please give it to me?" Some generous person in the crowd came up and handed me a copy of the book. With the book in my hand, I said, "Jesse Jackson, stand up!"

Jesse stood, and I said, "I've got a book for you. You are going to need it." I handed him the book and said, "Anybody who runs for president from any party is going to go through tough times."

Jesse took the book and accepted the gesture of friendship in the spirit in which it was intended. He laughed with everyone else, for he knew it was true—anyone running for president would be subject to tough times. They would have to face criticism, distortions, misinterpretations, and accusations. I tell you, many of the best people never run for political office because they don't want to go through the toughness of the campaign.

Think of All You Know

I have a grandson, Jason. Now with all modesty, I have to say Jason is a gifted, exceptional child. Yet when he was six months old, he couldn't do much. He couldn't take a spoon in his hand and dip it in a bowl of cereal, aim it at his mouth and hit it. He couldn't say "grandpa" or even his own name. He couldn't hold a pencil or control the movement of his own tiny fingers. He didn't know the difference between red and blue, and furthermore, he couldn't stand on his own two feet.

So if you find me an independent human being who has learned to stand on his own, speak proper sentences, button buttons and zip zippers, and write real letters, then you have found someone who is a borderline genius. Stop and realize all you have already learned in your lifetime. With so much going for you, you can do anything you set your mind to do. You are a brilliant human being. Some of the biggest goals you now have, along with the biggest problems you need to solve, are nothing compared to what you have already accomplished.

A Loss of Dignity

One day my wife and I were invited out to breakfast. It was held in a beautiful dining room. We were very impressed with the restaurant, and then we noticed a distinguished gentleman who came and sat in the booth next to us. He was elegantly dressed. His choice of clothes, shirt, tie, and hairstyle made him stand out as an impeccable gentleman. He was barely seated when he uttered a sentence that included about five words which I can only describe as the kind of language even an angry farmer wouldn't use in his barnyard. His style of dress and his bearing contradicted the words that came from his mouth. Suddenly the perspective we had of the gentleman was completely changed. He demeaned himself. He robbed himself of all dignity. When he first made an entrance into the dining room, he attracted attention because of a nobility in his bearing, an elegance in his manner. He wiped out all of his gain in one sweeping, careless, crude sentence. Words are powerful things, and you can't play lightly with them.

Ever Changing

I learned something interesting from Richard Neutra, one of the great architects of our century. When we retained him to build our first church building he said, "You know, one of the problems with buildings is, buildings are things, and things go out of style. Why? Because they don't grow, they don't change. They are static and people are bored with them.

"But," he added, "I have a solution to that problem. Dr. Schuller, people will never get bored with the buildings I'll build for you, because they'll see right through them. They'll see the sky and the trees. Some days, when they look out, the sky will be a drab gray. On other days, it'll be a bright blue, and some days it will be awash with splashes of white clouds. If they come in the nighttime, they may see a star or the moon. The building will be dynamic, exciting, and always changing."

A Great Attitude

Jesus Christ was the most positive Person who ever lived. Nothing is greater than meeting positive people. One summer I was in China and I met a vivacious eighty-three-year-old lady from Arkansas. She was a charming, delightful, positive person. I commented on how enthusiastic she was. "Oh, yes, Dr. Schuller," she said. "Ever since I began watching 'Hour of Power,' I've become so positive. You should know that at my age I have four boyfriends." She continued, "I begin my day with 'Will Power,' then I take a walk with 'Arthur Ritis,' come back with 'Charlie Horse,' and I spend my evening with 'Ben Gay.' " Now that's what I call positive thinking!

The Innermost Sanctum

Recently it was my joy to be invited to the home of Gregory Peck in Los Angeles, because Mr. Peck was doing the narration for the Glory of Easter which was to be staged in the Crystal Cathedral. Mr. Peck has always been my favorite actor. He is so elegant, so intelligent, so suave, charming, very honest, and kind.

Well, I had never been to his home before and like many of the homes in Bel Air or Beverly Hills, it's a marvelous place. Since it is hidden behind steel fences and steel gates, you can get only a glimpse of the house from the road. We announced our arrival, the gates swung open, we were admitted, and there was the beautiful house. We entered into the lovely home and were led into the living room. From there you could overlook the garden and the lawn.

I could have left that place and said that I was in Gregory Peck's private place. But I would have made a mistake. I was only in the living room—the front room of the main house.

It is at that level, however, that many of you people probably judge this ministry and the message that we're trying to get across. If you see the possibility thinking, that's only part of it. That's like saying, "Oh, I understand what he's

27

trying to say," when you've only been in the living room. That's because possibility thinking is only the centerpiece of the message. The story, the essence of Schuller and what he believes, doesn't end there.

Just before I left Mr. Peck, he said, "Bob, would you like to see where I do my work?"

I said, "Yes, I'd love to!"

As some of you know, Gregory Peck is recording the entire Bible for us. I had assumed he was doing the recording in the studio in Hollywood. Instead, when I asked him about it, he said, "Oh, I do it right here. I have a studio set up in a little log cabin here on my grounds. Let me show it to you."

So, we took a trip through the garden on the four-acre estate. We wound our way down the hillside until we came to a very secure, very secluded, very private ravine. There sits his log cabin. For all the world it is a log cabin like the one that Abraham Lincoln might have lived in. It was one room with very unpretentious furniture.

That's where Gregory Peck does his work. That's where he researches his roles and memorizes his lines, and that's where he is recording the Bible for us. Now that's the innermost sanctum where the work happens.

Today, I want to take you down a narrow little road to the log cabin where Schuller is really at. When you get there, we'll end up in a Bible verse. It is my favorite Bible verse. It is, "By grace are you saved, through faith, and not of yourself. It is a gift of God" (*see* Ephesians 2:8).

A Very Obvious Contradiction

Life is full of contradictions. Perhaps you have felt like the victim of an injustice. If so, you are not alone. There is much more of that in our society than we'd like to admit. I felt it myself recently. My publisher had sent me on a book tour, which means I had to fly around and meet the press at different points of the country. So it was that I found myself in Miami Beach. Since I was scheduled to be there only one night, I decided to call my friend Eddie Balestero. I called him and said, "Eddie, this is Dr. Schuller. What are you doing tomorrow?"

He said, "Not much, why?"

"Well," I said, "my publisher has rented a Lear Jet to take me from Florida to Washington, D.C., and we've got a couple of empty seats. Have you ever flown in a Lear Jet?"

"No."

"Well, then, why don't you come along with me tomorrow?"

The next day, Eddie and I were about thirty-five thousand feet up in the air in this Lear Jet. I said, "Why don't you give your wife a call?"

So Eddie called his wife. By this time he was having quite an exciting day. We landed at the airport. Waiting for me there was a huge limousine, again at the publisher's expense. Eddie got in the backseat of the limousine. He said, "This is the first time I've ever ridden in a limousine."

It was about noon. I said to the driver, "Louie, can you recommend a good place to have lunch?"

Louie said, "Oh, yes, Dr. Schuller, there's a restaurant I think you'd like. It's private and people won't bother you there."

I said, "Let's give it a try."

The day had been exhilarating until we ran into the snobbish maître d' in the restaurant. I said to him, "I'd like a table for two, please."

"Do you have a reservation?"

"No, but—"

"I'm sorry, we just don't have any space."

Just then I felt a hand on my back and a gusty voice said, "Bob Schuller, how are you?"

It was Fritz Mondale!

I said, "Oh, fine, Mr. Vice President. How are you? Meet my friend Eddie Balestero."

By this time, Eddie's head was spinning. We had a wonderful conversation. The maître d' said, "Your table is ready, Mr. Vice President."

And then he looked at me and said, "Oh, I just noticed that we do have another table."

So Eddie and I had lunch. Contradiction—one moment no tables at all. The next moment, we had a table.

An Enormous Success

When he was forty-six years of age, Oscar Hammerstein had worked with thirty different composers. Nothing took off. There was no successful song. It was a despairing, dispiriting time for him. Finally, Oscar Hammerstein tied in with Richard Rodgers. The following year they wrote the musical *Oklahoma*. He was a success. In fact his success was so enormous in its impact that he went out and bought a full page ad in *Variety* magazine. To keep himself humble, he bought this headline: "I've done it before and I can do it again!" He then listed every single one of his failures.

A Fictitious General

I love the story of the man who was very insecure. One day he was promoted from major to colonel and was ushered into his new office. He looked proudly at his new surroundings and sat in the chair. Suddenly there was a knock at the door. He said, "Come in." In walked a corporal. The colonel said, "Just a minute, I have to finish this phone call." He picked up the receiver, pushed the button, and said, "I'm sorry about the interruption, General. Now, where were we? Oh, yes sir, I will take care of it. Of course I will, sir. It's true we are close friends. Yes, I'll call the president immediately after I finish talking with you, General. You're welcome, sir." The colonel ceremoniously put the phone down, turned to the corporal, and asked, "What can I do for you?" He answered, "Well, sir, I just came in to connect your telephone."

One of My Biggest Mistakes

I attended a tiny country high school in Iowa. I never took geometry. When I started my undergraduate studies at Hope College, Michigan, I discovered that everyone was required to take eight hours of science. Math courses are applicable to that requirement.

Consequently, I was put into a math course. The first week the professor rattled off some statements. He was referring to geometric principles. Because I'd never had geometry, I didn't know what he was talking about. But I noticed that the other students were nodding as if they completely understood. I did as they did, thinking, *I'll pick it up later.* The next week it was the same. I didn't have the foggiest notion what he was talking about, but I pretended that I understood it as clearly as my fellow students did. The truth of the matter showed on my first test. I didn't get a good grade.

My professor approached me and kindly asked, "Are you having problems, Bob?" I said, "Oh, no. I'm doing just fine." That was a lie. If I were completely honest I would have admitted that I had an enormous gap and lack in my precollege work. But I didn't want to admit it because I didn't want him to know how dumb I was. That was one of the biggest mistakes I ever made.

If I had only known what I'm trying to teach you now— that if there is a gap, a lack, or a need, have enough spirit to admit where you are poor—I could have gone to him for help. I could have pulled an *A* instead of a *D*.

What's Your Need?

I remember years ago, when E. Stanley Jones used to conduct *ashrams,* as he called them. *Ashram* is a term used in India. It means a time of spiritual growth and expansion. Dr. Jones always began his ashrams by passing out pieces of paper with this introduction: "No one will see what you are about to write on this paper. I want you to write what your need is today."

It happened at every ashram. While people were thinking and praying and writing, someone would say, "Brother Stanley, I don't have a need. What do you write down, if you don't have a need?" And Brother Stanley would say, "If you think you don't have a need, then *that's* your need!"

EXTRAORDINARY ATTITUDE

The Power to Control

Not long ago I had an unforgettable experience. I have a friend who recently bought a new Cessna Citation jet airplane. When he invited me to lunch I jokingly said, "Good, let's go have lunch in Cabo San Lucas."

He took me seriously! So the other morning we left at 6:30 A.M. for Cabo San Lucas, at the tip of Baja California. Now, on Cabo San Lucas, there's the beautiful Finistera Hotel that lies on the ridge between two huge rocks. As we approached our destination, my friend said to his copilot, "Will you trade places with Dr. Schuller?" I must tell you that I am not a pilot. I've never had my hands on the controls of a plane.

My friend said, "Bob, you're a possibility thinker." I said, "Yes."

"Okay, I want you to take the controls of this jet, and in a few minutes you'll fly us right in to Cabo San Lucas. Come in low, and go right between those rocks. Then curve and go over the bay, where we'll dip the wings over the boat waiting for us."

I gulped and said, "Sure, I'd love to do it." I put my hands on the controls and followed his instructions. It was incredibly simple. As easy as putting melted butter on a hot bun, I flew that plane right over the hotel and cleanly between the rocks. It's a tremendous feeling, having the power to control the direction of such a plane.

Similarly, you have the power to control your life and your prosperity. You even have the power to turn your poverty into prosperity. You can get what you really need, and want, if you'll do it God's way.

This morning, I want you to imagine that you are in a jet airplane. You're putting your hands on the controls for the first time, and you're steering this magnificent flying creature. What potential you have!

37

Beginning Is Half Done

Some of you may be afraid to begin. You don't think you can finish. You're thinking, *Can I make it all the way to the top?* Here's a great concept: Just decide to begin and then decide to keep going. Don't worry about the top—just decide to keep going past the point of no return. That's all you do. That's the way I do it.

A couple of days ago I knew I had to run. I wanted to run. I knew I should run. But I wasn't in the mood for running the six miles I usually run. My home is six miles from the church, so I got into my running suit and decided, "I'm only going to run halfway from the house to the church." When I got halfway from the house to the church, what could I do? I couldn't hitchhike home. I had to finish; there was no other way.

I use this principle a lot in my life. When I know there is something that I should do but don't want to do the whole thing, I only make the commitment to go as far as the point of no return. Then I'm trapped. I have to complete the job. The key is in deciding to begin.

A Desire to Succeed

Dear Dr. Schuller,

Last year I made a decision to return to college. I'm thirty-four years old. I have four children. I really doubted my decision because I had been dismissed from another college at the age of nineteen for poor grades. I was especially afraid of algebra, which I had failed flat. But in May of last year, having moved to Texas many years ago, I heard that you were speaking at the American Renewal Series in Dallas. I was once a member of the Garden Grove Community Church and thought your message might give me a lift. Perhaps I could even make a new resolution and follow through if I got motivated. So I drove into Dallas and heard the story you told about the man who failed college and went on to become a doctor who was the attendant of Bobby Kennedy.

Dr. Schuller, I know I was not the only person in that convention center, but that message was for me. I decided that, despite my terrible academic record, I would go back to school. I did, and I completed the year with a 4.0 average, including two algebra classes. That's pretty good for somebody who flunked out of Fullerton fifteen years ago. Thank you, Dr. Schuller.

Floyd Baker's Faith in Teaching

Floyd Baker, a friend of mine, teaches physics and astronomy at Fullerton College. It was many years ago when Floyd started coming to our church. He began listening to the lectures and messages on positive thinking and self-esteem psychology. As he heard the principles on faith and positive programming, he wondered, *Will this work in my college classroom?* At that time, every year 50 percent of the students who took the Introduction to Physics for Science Majors course at Fullerton College flunked, and consequently, every year in his first lecture he'd say, "I want to be honest with you. This is probably the toughest course you'll ever take. Fifty percent of you will flunk. It happens every year." He was right. Fifty percent of them always flunked.

However, after listening to the messages in our church he decided to try a most audacious experiment. He stood before his incoming class and said, "Students, I have to tell you something. This introductory course in physics is very difficult. In fact, fifty percent of the students have failed this course every year. But I've been checking your records and I'm impressed with you. I am amazed at what an unbelievable class this is. You are all tremendously bright. In fact, I predict that for the first time in the history of this school, all of you will pass. None of you will flunk."

Later he confessed to me that it was terrribly frightening to make such a claim. However, he reported in a paper the following results: "I did not change my testing procedures one bit. And that year, every student in that class passed.

Not one failed. I know I worked harder as a teacher, and the students did also."

I can do all things if . . . I am programmed positively. The Bible calls it faith. We call it possibility thinking. Even Jesus said that you could move mountains, on one condition: you must have faith.

Nobody can begin to understand the power of faith. We don't know how it works, but once you have a positive picture in your mind and you hold it before you, unseen, unmeasurable, and undetectable forces are released. These forces—call them determination if you will—can bring success to anyone who believes. I can do all things if . . . I have the faith. That is the first condition.

The Best Man for the Job

There once was a king who needed to hire a carriage driver. He decided to test the applicants for the job by asking them to drive the carriage as fast as they could, and as close to the edge of a cliff as they could, without endangering the life of the occupant. He watched as some sped by only three feet away from the cliff. Each applicant, trying to outdo the other, drove closer and closer to the edge. Finally, it was the last man's turn. He surprised everyone by slowly driving down the middle of the road.

When the king made his choice, whom do you think he picked? He chose the man who drove down the middle of the road. Why? When the king asked the last driver, "Why did you drive down the middle of the road?" the carriage driver said, "I believe in staying as far away from danger as possible. That's the way I'll drive if you hire me."

How do you handle life's temptations? Avoid them. Avoid the spills. But what if you've already made one big mistake? You still live above your circumstances and not under them.

Turn Your Problem Inside Out

A psychiatrist once told me about a counseling session he had had with a certain patient. He said, "After listening to the patient for a long time, I told him, 'I noticed that there are two words you use all the time. Those two words are the cause of your emotional depression. Wipe those two words out of your vocabulary and you'll never have to come to me again. The two words are: *if only.* Wipe them out. They make you sick. In their place substitute these two words: *next time.*' "

Don't curse your hurts. Don't nurse them. Don't rehearse them. Disperse them. How do you disperse them? As Max Cleland, author of *Strong at the Broken Places,* stated, you can disperse your hurts by looking for another open door. When you look for the open doors, your back is to the closed door. And every time one door closes, God opens another one. You disperse your hurt when you reverse it. Reversing it means you turn it inside out. You turn the problem into a partner. You turn the scar into a star. You turn your frustrations into a fruitful experience.

Consider Tomorrow

Recently, while in New York to deliver a message, I took a cab from downtown Manhattan to Long Island. During the hour-long ride I worked on the message I was to give. I took out my daily itinerary for the three-day visit to the city and began to make notes on the back.

I looked over the notes I'd written. I was dissatisfied with them. In my frustration I tore the page off, threw it down, and started over. I wrote down new thoughts on the next page of my itinerary. My new efforts were better.

When I reached my destination I began to get out of the car. Suddenly I remembered the piece of paper I'd crumpled and thrown on the floor. That paper contained my itinerary for the next day. I said, "Hey, I've got to keep that." As I retrieved my itinerary I added, "I almost threw away part of tomorrow."

Shoes for Africa

Life is a matter of perspective. Consider, for instance, the story of the two shoe salesmen who were sent to Africa to check into the potential international market there. Like the two spies who returned to Joshua in the Old Testament after reviewing the Promised Land, the salesmen returned to their shoe company with their report. One salesman had a negative report. "There is no market there," he said. "Nobody wears shoes in Africa." The positive salesman reported, "On the contrary, it's a fantastic opportunity—no one has bought shoes yet!"

Life is a matter of perspective and life's perspective is a self-fulfilling prophecy.

Build a Bigger Island

I've made six trips to Japan in the past fifteen years and on one of those trips I said to a group of pastors, "You need a larger piece of property on which you can build a bigger church."

But they replied, "Dr. Schuller, you don't understand. When you live on an island, you cannot grow." Their answer sounded so profound at the time, but something about it bothered me. Finally I figured out why that statement bothered me. I know from having visited the Netherlands that any country that borders on the ocean is expandable. In Holland, they just built the dyke and siphoned off the water. The ocean was pushed farther back, and today they've got a bigger country without going to war or threatening a neighbor.

Here's what you can learn from this: As a human being, you are an island of consciousness with boundaries of awareness that limit your knowledge and understanding. However, you can move the island until it is bigger.

This business of expanding your consciousness is not an option. Either you are expandable or you are expendable. What do I mean? When you stop growing, you start dying—intellectually, spiritually, emotionally, and professionally.

Give It Your Best

Dr. Herman Ridder was with me at West Point one day and the cadets were so enthusiastic. They were getting ready to win their five-hundredth game in hockey. Can you imagine? But Dr. Ridder had a marvelous observation. He said, "If you have five hundred straight wins you're in the wrong league."

It's true. If you keep winning, winning, winning, then you're really losing, because you're not facing an adequate opponent.

Some people handle contradictions by simply resisting them. In Birmingham, Alabama, they tell the story about a great football game. The teams were really unequally matched. One was made up of little guys and the other had big guys. It was a scary game for the little guys. As you might guess, they were losing, but miraculously, only by one touchdown. With only a few minutes to go, the coach called them all together. He said to the quarterback, "Loo, we can win this game. We're little, but Calhoun can run faster than anybody. Give the ball to Calhoun."

Back on the field, it was time for the first play. Calhoun did not get the ball. The coach, on the sidelines, was very upset. On play two, Calhoun still didn't get the ball. The game ended. They lost. The coach said, "Why didn't you give the ball to Calhoun?"

The quarterback said, "Calhoun wouldn't take the ball!"

Is your name Calhoun? Mine? Do you look at the big guys, at the mountains, and hope they'll go away if you ignore them?

Perhaps you don't dare to sell your product because you

don't want to be rejected. Are you so afraid of failure that you never try?

Remember, truth is the center of the intersection. The truth is that you won't succeed until you've had a failure. Only then will you know you've given it your best. Really, that's what success is all about.

"Hit It to Me!"

I don't know anybody who practices possibility thinking better than Tommy Lasorda.

I remember asking him once, "Tommy, how can you constantly keep your enthusiasm up? You lose some, you win some. How do you keep your enthusiasm up? How do you keep ringing the bell, getting a dream again?"

He said, "Oh, I just constantly welcome ideas that challenge the impossible."

I asked, "How do you inspire your guys?"

He said, "Let me give you this illustration: One time we were really doing pretty poorly. I noticed the guys weren't fielding very well. Too many hits were getting by. So I did something we had never done before. I gathered the players together in the locker room and I said to them, 'Let's pretend it's a tight game. We're ahead four to three. It's the last half of the ninth. We're still leading by one run. Bases are loaded. There are two outs. Suddenly a heavy hitter comes to bat. You are all out there in the field. Question: What do you think?' They all said, 'Tommy, we think, *I hope he doesn't hit it to me!*'"

Tommy's reply? "That's the trouble! In a tight spot, you go back out there and you think, *Hey, hit it to me! I want it!*"

Anything's Possible

Recently I lectured in Seattle, Washington, where I met a fellow who was six feet four inches tall and broad-shouldered. He was grinning from ear to ear and had a lovely wife at his side.

He said, "Dr. Schuller I can't begin to thank you. That stuff you dish out every Sunday really works. I didn't believe in Christianity but my wife did, and she made me watch the 'Hour of Power.' I started watching, then I started listening, and finally the things you were saying really seemed to make sense. To make a long story short, today I'm a Christian!"

Then he said, "That's not all. After I became a Christian, I decided to practice faith—or as you call it—possibility thinking. And I've gotta tell you—it works! You won't believe what it did for me. I had read in the paper here in Seattle that there was going to be a fishing tournament. They tagged a few salmon and whoever caught the tagged salmon would win the jackpot of one million dollars!"

He continued, "Dr. Schuller, I caught the salmon with the tag! However, before the tournament was ended, one other guy caught a tagged fish, so I have to split the million with the other guy. But, I'm getting twenty-five thousand dollars a year for the next twenty years!"

He was so excited. He added, "It would not have happened if I hadn't become a possibility thinker and thought that it might be possible to catch the fish."

Get Set for a Long Life

Rene Dubos, a great scientist who died not too long ago, said, "The human being has an infinite capacity to adjust downward," to which I replied, "Adjustment is always a downward movement. The upward movement is never an adjustment—it is always a commitment!" That commitment comes through self-esteem, pride, and human worth.

To my knowledge, the last article written by Rene Dubos was in the December issue of *Omni* magazine. It was called "Survival," and in it he said what I'm trying to say. If you lose your pride in being human, you lose your self-esteem. When that happens you'll no longer believe that it's possible to solve the problems. Self-esteem produces possibility thinking. Remove self-dignity and you remove self-confidence. But adopt the faith of your Father's possibility thinking, and then get set for a surprise.

Take Another Look

A while back I was at Knott's Berry Farm. I hadn't been there for years. They still sell a complete chicken dinner for $6.50. I read the menu and was reminded of their inspiring story. It was during the big depression. Walter Knott, his wife, Cordelia, and their four children could not make ends meet. So Cordelia started making a couple of extra jars of jelly. She'd make extra pies and put them out on a rickety card table by the road. She'd wave down passersby who stopped to buy her wares. This worked so well that she added a couple of pieces of chicken. She put up a sign, offering a chicken dinner for only a couple of dollars.

Through such efforts, Cordelia kept that family together. She turned the depression into a launching pad. Be positive. Take another look. There are always possibilities.

Play With Your Dream

It's amazing, when you take the attitude of fun, how often you can perform so much better. I was excited when Debbie Armstrong won a gold medal in the 1984 Winter Olympics. I think the secret of her success was her attitude. Kristin Cooper, her teammate, said, "Debbie and I were up at the top and she was laughing and babbling away. She kept saying, 'We're just going to have fun. We're just going to go down that mountain and have fun. You have a good run, Cooper, but just have fun.' And when she stomped out of that chute, I couldn't believe her."

Let's just have fun! In talking about her success later, Debbie said, "I always knew that if I got my head in gear, and just got up there on that mountain and was happy and had fun, I would do well."

I must confess—most of my dreams started out as jokes. There was a time when I said, "We're going to build a new church. Let's just make it a great big glass box." A lot of us laughed about it. Play with your dream. Have fun.

The Best Way to Start a Day

One morning I was sitting in a restaurant with my wife, having an early-morning cup of coffee, away from home, away from the telephone, where we could put ourselves together and plan our day. An elderly man came and sat in the adjoining booth. The waitress came and poured him coffee. As she poured him his first cup of coffee she said, "That's the best way to start a day, with a good cup of coffee." And he said, "Oh, no, the best way to start a day is not with a good cup of coffee, but the best way to start a day is with a—"

He stopped, smiled, and his eyes twinkled as he said, "The best way to start a day is with a good morning." And I was so proud to observe that he was a member of our church. A Christian is basically positive instead of basically negative. Yes, the best way to start a day is with a good morning!

"You Really Gave Me a Boost!"

I received a telephone call one morning just before I went into the pulpit. The call was from Vince Evans, quarterback for the Chicago Bears. Vince came to Jesus Christ one Easter morning while watching the "Hour of Power." He called to ask me to pray for him and his team. They were playing one of the most important games of the season. "Dr. Schuller," Vince began, "today we're playing Tampa. Tampa's good. Some say nobody can beat them. I want to do the very best I can. Will you pray with me?"

"Of course I'll pray with you, Vince," I said. And I began by thanking God for the beautiful human bodies He created. I thanked God for Vince's clear mind—a mind that was unpolluted by drugs or chemicals. And I thanked God for the dynamic spirit that was shaping Vince's life. As we came to the close of our prayer together, I prayed, "Oh, Lord, when he takes off the football helmet and steps into the shower, may he have the wonderful feeling that comes with knowing he played straight, honest, and the best he could."

"You really gave me a boost!" Vince said after we prayed. "You know," I answered, "you gave me a boost, too!" "I did?" he asked. "How did I give you a boost?" "Well," I responded, "for years, I've been sitting in my office on the twelfth floor of the Tower of Hope. For years I've sat at this desk and looked at the wallpaper. The designs are shaped kind of like parachutes. But as I was talking to you I suddenly realized that they're not parachute-shaped after all—

51

they're shaped like football helmets!" "But how does that give you a boost?" Vince persisted.

"From now on, every time I sit here pondering a problem, formulating answers to questions, making decisions, climbing mountains, and overcoming obstacles, I'll look at those helmets and think of you and the other great football players I know. I'll think of how you 'Go, go, go,' and 'Win, win, win!' "

Freedom From the Bayou

A group of women who lived on the bayou were complaining because they didn't live in the city and didn't have luxurious homes. One of the women was a positive thinker. She got so tired of the other complainers, the faultfinders, and the criticizers that she finally looked at them and said, "Look, you live on the bayou. The bayou flows into the ocean. You've got a boat. You can go anywhere from where you are."

When you begin to believe in God, it's like having a house on the bayou, because God, like the bayou, flows into the gulf, and the gulf flows into the river, the river flows into the ocean, and there's no end to it. So there is no end to God's power and God's possibilities to do something within you. And when you touch faith with God, it's like living on the bayou. You can go anywhere from where you are.

Labor Made Easier

Two laborers were watching a new computerized steam shovel at work in an open pit mine. The shovel took in a truckload of dirt in one big bite. After just a few bites the truck was full. One laborer said to the other, "Man, that machine has put five hundred of us out of work. It's our enemy!" The other man said, "Yes, and if we got rid of our shovels, we could create a million jobs for people to dig the mine with spoons."

You Choose to Succeed or Fail

I talked to a businessman who said, "I've failed but it's not my fault." And do you know why he said that? Because he blamed his failure on everybody else! He attacked the unions, governmental regulations, the tax structure, and competition. And I had to say to him as friendly and yet as firmly as I could, "Sir, in the final analysis you threw in the towel, they didn't. You said, 'I give up.' You decided to quit." And at that point he finally admitted, "I guess I did."

I suspect that at the end of my life somebody may say,

"Schuller was a big failure . . . in golf!" And that's true! I used to play golf but I was so terrible I gave it up! I quit! Someone might also say that I was a failure in tennis. And that would be true, too! But I have chosen to be a failure in these sports. Instead, I have chosen to divert my time and energies to other areas. You succeed or fail based on the decisions you make!

A Matter of Outlook

I've been on university campuses and I've seen a lot of young people, eighteen, nineteen, and twenty years of age. Many of them walk slowly. They move in a fatigued way. They slouch in their chairs. They have an extremely low level of energy. Yet, I can show you people in our church, like my Uncle Henry, who is in his ninetieth year, who has a spring in his step. He's difficult to keep up with.

It's not a matter of the calendar. It's a matter of outlook. The energy you have depends upon your mood, and your moods depend on the thoughts you entertain.

You Have Wisdom

There's a story about a man from the Orient who traveled around the world in search of the smartest guru. He was told that the wise old man lived in a cave high up in the Himalayas, so that was his final destination. He loaded his horse down with supplies and set off across the mountains and deserts to find this man of wisdom. After months of traveling, he came to the foot of the Himalayas. He led his horse up a narrow path until he came to a cave. "Are you the guru who is known for his wisdom around the world?" he called out.

He waited and waited until finally the old man walked out into the light, so that he could be seen. "Old man, how can I become brilliant? Where can I find wisdom?" the weary traveler asked. The wise old guru raised his head and looked into the anxious man's eyes. "Where can you find your horse?" And with that he turned and walked back into the dark cave.

His horse was with him all the time! Brilliance and the capacity for wisdom were with him all the time. It's right there deep inside of you. Jesus said, "The kingdom of God is within you" (Luke 17:21). God is sending ideas to you that can take the form of dreams, but you don't believe it! You have that ability! You have that gift!

Teamwork

No one can operate successfully in isolation. Dare to share the credit and glory with a winning team. History is inveterate in its teaching. Ultimately only teams will succeed.

Zig Ziglar once said, "If tomorrow you got a call from your boss and he said to you, 'Hey, I have good news for you. I have free tickets for you and your wife to Acapulco. You leave two weeks from today and we will provide full air fare, all your meals, rooms in the best hotel, and a five-hundred-dollar bonus to make sure you have plenty of tipping money,' what would you do? You wouldn't say, 'Sorry, sir, I wasn't planning on it.' You know what you'd do. You'd get organized in a hurry and rearrange your schedule. You'd do everything in your power to make it possible for you to go. You would begin to delegate some jobs that yesterday you thought you, and you alone, could do. You would start giving somebody else some of the power and glory that you possess today."

I am a success in my life, my marriage, my family, and in my career simply because I am surrounded by better, wiser people than myself. Those of you who watch the "Hour of Power" on television may know only me and my son, but in this church there are a thousand or more laypersons who make this program possible.

Eliminate Your Negative Thoughts

One winter I took a trip up the Nile River to Aswan Dam. In the old tomb of the kings there are sketches of the pharaohs. It was fascinating to learn that every representation of pharaohs in the temples depicted the pharaoh with a bird and a snake around his head. The bird is a vulture, and the snake is a wrapped cobra. The vulture eats rotten food and the cobra attacks and kills.

These symbolized that the pharaoh had to guard the thoughts that went on in his head. If rotten thoughts came, the vulture would consume them, and if poisonous thoughts came, the cobra would kill them.

We're taught from childhood that you don't hit, you don't kill, you don't steal, and you don't lie. In the same way, we should teach children from infancy on that you do not allow negative thoughts to enter your head and when they do, you should, like a cobra, kill those thoughts.

Turn the Dial on Your Crummy Moods

Every morning before my children left for school, my family and I would repeat the lines of Ella Wheeler Wilcox: "I'm going to be happy today." How you are going to feel today is a decision you make. As our children were growing up we taught them a cybernetic reality, and that is, the brain is like a radio dial. All of the ideas that bombard you are like sound waves. You can switch the dial and pick up music, or you can pick up propaganda, or you can pick up some tension-producing message. We say to our kids, "Turn the dial." If they get depressed or cynical or crabby or grumbling, we tell them, "Come on, turn the dial." Make the choice that is positive. Choose to feel good today.

Now, if you think that's too simplistic and unsophisticated, consider the findings in a recently published book by David D. Burns, M.D., Professor of Psychiatry, at the University of Pennsylvania. His book is called *Feeling Good*. What is he talking about? He is stating that the most important thing in life is to feel good and have emotionally healthy feelings on a day-to-day basis. Feelings will control everything. You can bury a stick; you can bury a tin can; you can bury a stone or a bone; you can bury a piece of glass—but you cannot bury a worm. And you can't just bury your feelings. That is a psychological impossibility, because feelings will either peek out or shriek out. You can't ignore them. You have to deal with them.

It's a lot harder to harness the exit of an emotion than it is to control the entrance of an emotion. It's much more difficult to control your temper than it is to prevent yourself from anger in the first place. It's much easier to feel good on a daily basis when positive emotions are fed upon every day.

"My Name Is Phideaux"

The story comes to mind of the two sophisticated, snobbish French poodles who ran into a mongrel on the corner. The mongrel said to the poodles, "What are your names?"

One Poodle said, "My name is Mimi, M-i-m-i."

And the other said, "My name is Fifi, F-i-f-i."

And the mongrel said, "My name is Fido, P-h-i-d-e-a-u-x!"

Contradictions. They are in all of life. The trick is to combine them creatively. When we do, then we make the lion lie down with the lamb.

Your Key for Success

A psychologist and I were talking about a person we were both interested in trying to help. This person's whole life was one set of problems—one failure after another—and each failure reinforced the future failure. That's why you call people like him "born losers." The psychologist hit it right on the head. He said, "The trouble is this person has never had a peak experience." He's never had an experience in really succeeding. So he's convinced that he was born a failure. This young man failed in school, failed in teenage relationships, failed in sociological relationships, failed in his first job, got fired from his second job, and landed in a reform school. And that's basically his life-style. His last peak experience was when he learned to walk!

How can you have a peak experience? There is no way it can happen without the kind of dynamic, religious experience we call "establishing a relationship with God." And that is the key.

EXTRAORDINARY HUMOR

King of the Jungle

A lion was king of the jungle. One day as he paraded through the jungle he met a rabbit. He said, "Who is the king of the jungle?" The rabbit said, "You are." Next the lion came to a deer and asked the elegant creature, "Who is the king of the jungle?" The deer said, "You are, Mr. Lion." So he walked on and met a tall giraffe, towering higher than all of the creatures in the jungle. The lion looked up to the giraffe and roared, "Who is the king of the jungle?" The giraffe bowed his head, bent his neck, until his eyes were even with the lion, and said, "You are, Mr. Lion."

Proudly, the beast went on his way until he ran into a huge bull elephant with tusks six feet long. He looked up at the monstrous creature and roared, "Who is the king of the jungle?" The elephant, without saying a word, swung his trunk back and forth, wrapped it around the lion's body, lifted him up, whirled him around, then slapped him against the side of a mountain. The lion, dazed, struggled to his feet, staggered over to the elephant, and said, "Just because you didn't know the answer, you don't have to get so mad."

A Three-Legged Chicken

Bob Hope tells a story about a fellow who was riding along at fifty-five miles an hour when he looked out the window. He couldn't believe his eyes! He saw a three-legged chicken running right alongside the car! He increased his speed to sixty miles an hour but the chicken kept right up with him. At seventy miles an hour, the chicken took off and left the man behind in a cloud of dust. Dumbfounded, the man pulled over and stopped in a farmer's yard. He rolled down his window and asked the farmer who was sitting there, "Did you see that?" The farmer said, "Sure, I saw it. I've seen plenty of them."

The man said, "What was it?"

"That was just one of our three-legged chickens."

"Three-legged chicken! What do you mean a three-legged chicken?"

"Well," the farmer said, "there are three of us in the family: my wife, my boy, and myself. We all like drumsticks. So we decided to breed a three-legged chicken. That way, we all get a drumstick."

Plan Ahead

When I was in Washington recently, President Reagan made an interesting comment. He referred to Abraham, who lived to be nearly 150 years old. His wife was only a few years younger. The president said, "Can you imagine how rich he would have been if he'd opened an IRA account?"

Mixed-Up Messages

Recently I heard about a florist who was going out of business. Someone said the reason he failed was that he always got his messages mixed up. You see, a terrible thing happened one time. He was told to send flowers to a newly married couple. The florist also had an order to send flowers for a local funeral.

Well, he got the cards mixed up! The people who were getting married got the message "Our deepest sympathy to both of you." At the funeral, they got the message "Good luck in your new location."

The Spanish Monk

I remember the story of the monk who went into a monastery in Spain. One of the requirements of the religious order is that the monks must maintain perpetual silence. Only after two years are the monks allowed to speak, and then only two words. And then, after two years of additional silence, they're allowed two more words, and so it goes every two years. There was a young man who had spent his first two years at the monastery and then was called by his superior to make his first two-word statement. His first two words were, "Bed hard." Two years passed and he got his second chance. His next two words were, "Food bad." Two more years passed. His two words were: "I quit!" The superior looked at him and said, "It doesn't surprise me. All you've done since you've been here is complain, complain, complain."

A Local Call

There is a humorous story making the rounds in Washington about the time Menachem Begin met with President Reagan. He was curious about the three telephones on

President Reagan's desk. Reagan explained, "Well, the silver one connects me to the USSR, the platinum one connects me to the Republican headquarters, and the gold one connects me to God." Begin said, "Really? What does it cost to use the gold phone?" The president replied, "Ten thousand dollars. But it's worth it." Not many weeks later, when Reagan visited Israel, guess what he saw on Begin's desk? Three phones: one silver, one platinum, one gold. When Reagan asked what they were for, Begin answered, "The silver one is for the head of the Israeli political party, and the gold one is my line to God." Reagan said, "Yeah, what does it cost to call God?" Begin exclaimed, "Oh, just ten cents—here it's a local call!"

Sister Theresa's Travels

I heard a cute story recently. God decided to send one of the righteous women to check out some of the problem spots in the world. He said to a nun, whose name was Sister Theresa, "I want you to go to New York City. Reports are that it's pretty bad. I'll give you a call and you can let me know."

She said, "Okay, I'll be at the Waldorf Astoria."

After a few days the Lord called her. She said, "Lord, it's worse than You've been told. The city is as decadent as Rome was at its worst."

God said, "I was afraid of that. Now I need you to go and check out Las Vegas."

She went to Las Vegas. She said. "You'll be able to reach me at the MGM Grand Hotel."

The Lord called her after a few days and she said, "Lord, it is worse than You've been told. It's like Sodom and Gomorrah."

God said, "Sister Theresa, I want you to check out one other place: Hollywood, California."

She said, "Okay. Try to reach me at the Beverly Hills Hotel."

After a few days, He called the Beverly Hills Hotel. The phone rang in her room. A tape recorder came on. "Hello, this is Terry, fer sure. I'll be back in thirty minutes."

Good News and Bad News

I recently heard the story of two great ball players—Dodgers, naturally. The two men made an agreement that whoever died first would return to communicate to the living friend whether or not there was baseball in heaven. The inevitable happened—one of them died shortly afterward. The surviving player sat in the dugout during a game one day, and suddenly in the third inning he felt himself surrounded by light. He knew immediately that it was his fellow teammate who had died. There in the dugout, the player heard a voice speaking to him: "Hey, it's me. I've got good news and bad news. The good news is there is baseball in heaven! I'm playing with Ty Cobb, Babe Ruth, and all the greats. It's fantastic! The bad news is I noticed you're scheduled to pitch next Tuesday!"

The Secret to Success

I have a story about a sea captain, a very successful sea captain. Everybody wanted to know what his secret was. They noticed that every morning right after breakfast he would go up to his cabin, draw the drapes, lock the door, and spend some time alone. He would then come out confident with intelligence, capable of coping with all of the pressures that a captain has to handle. And the second officers often wanted to know what he did that made him so strong, wise, and confident. Finally they devised a scheme so they could peek into the privacy of his cabin.

After breakfast the officers watched the captain go into his cabin, unlock the safe, and pull out an envelope. From the envelope he took a piece of paper which he put on the table and with his hand on his head, he read from the piece of paper. He looked and looked and looked. Then he put the paper back in the envelope, put it back in the safe, spun the cycle, locked it, came out confidently, and gave his commands. The ship sailed magnificently.

They checked on him day after day; every day it was the same routine. The drapes would be drawn, the door locked, the safe opened, and the envelope pulled out. That same piece of paper folded on the table. He would look and look and look.

The day came when the captain died. The officers rushed into his cabin, opened the safe, pulled out the envelope, looked at the paper, and saw his secret. There were the words: "The right-hand side is the starboard side."

EXTRAORDINARY PERSEVERANCE

A Thrill That Fulfills

Our daughter Carol is a skier. Last year she tried five times to qualify for the National Handicapped National Ski Championships. But she failed to ski fast enough without falling or something. Last week she had another opportunity to qualify. In order to do so you have to make the race in a certain time. In the first race she was disqualified because she lost her outriggers. In the second race, she felt she was too slow. And in the third race she went so fast that she ended up sitting down on the ski as she came across the line. That eliminated her from that race.

Assuming she had failed at all three attempts, she didn't wait for the results. She and her coach were in the locker room when they heard over the public-address system, "The winner of the second race, setting a speed qualifying her for the nationals and winning a gold medal, is Carol Schuller." She made it! But I must say, she really paid a high price for it.

I'm not talking in terms of dollars. I'm talking about one word: *effort.* You've got one life to live—don't spill it. Don't settle for a cheap thrill. Don't buy the frills. Sharpen the skills necessary to make your dream come true.

With that kind of character, you'll be on top of the circumstances, not under them. If you want to see it through, it is up to you. If you want to go from now to the end of your life, healthy, happy, and successful, then I say, if you want to see it through, it's up to you. Right now I ask you to do one thing. And that is this: Turn your whole life over to Jesus Christ. Your sins? He'll forgive them. Ideas? He'll give you some fantastic ones. If you follow them, you'll find a thrill that will really fulfill.

My First Dream

Do you know what my first dream was? The first dream I ever had came to me when I was a little boy and I began to scheme how I could accomplish it. I had the dream that I wanted to be a minister. And then I had to develop the scheme—it meant eight years of school, four years of high school, four years in college, and then three years in theological graduate school. That's nineteen years of education. And at the age of five I made that commitment.

Anything can be accomplished if you're willing to pay the price, prepare for it, and stick with the scheme: How much will it take? What will it cost? What kind of resources will I need? What kind of help will I need?

The Help of Rosie Gray

Our interest in the handicapped is not new. Actually, the ministry of the Crystal Cathedral was the result of one disabled person. Twenty-six years ago, when my wife and I came to California to begin a church, all I had was four hundred dollars and a dream. We couldn't find a chapel, empty hall, or school building to rent for Sunday worship. Finally, in desperation, we used a drive-in theater that stands only a mile from the Crystal Cathedral. From the platform of the snack bar roof, I preached to a few curious people who came in their cars. I prayed that the months would quickly pass and we could raise money, find land, build a chapel, and worship in a "civilized" Christian way.

Unknown to me, on the first Sunday at the drive-in, there was a totally paralyzed woman in the audience. Her husband, Warren Gray, had seen the ad in the local paper which was placed there by this twenty-eight-year-old minister: "Starting Sunday, March 27—Worship as you are, in the family car!" And the old rancher lifted Rosie, his seventy-two-year-old, paralyzed wife, carried her to the car, and drove her to that drive-in theater because it was the only church she could attend.

Years before, Rosie had had a stroke. She could not walk or talk or control her actions. By any indication, Rosie was totally out of it. The truth was, she had a clear mind and understood what she heard. Although the Grays came regularly, I never met Rosie and Warren until our congregation bought land and built a small chapel. We were ready to make the move out of the drive-in and into our new home, when Rosie's husband Warren asked me to call on them. Meeting me at the front door of their ranch home, he said, "Reverend, before you meet Rosie I must tell you that you may not think she has a brain. She can't walk. She can't talk. She had a stroke years ago, but she is actually smart. She and I have been attending the drive-in every week and we'd like to join the church." After this introduction, I met Rosie.

As I knelt by her bedside, I asked, "Rosie, do you love Jesus?" Without nodding her head or blinking her eyes, she answered my question as one small tear rolled down her cheek. The following Sunday she and her husband were received as charter members of the church. Meanwhile the congregation prepared to move into the little chapel with the new carpeting, upholstered pews, stained-glass windows, and beautiful woodwork.

Finally, after so many years, we would be out of the drive-in. Yet suddenly we had a problem—what would we do with Rosie Gray? She couldn't sit in a wheelchair. She either had to be strapped to a bed or to the seat of the car. So twenty-five years ago, confronted with the reality of the handicapped, we decided to conduct two church services each Sunday. At half-past nine we worshiped in our new little chapel. Then, following the first service, I dashed out to the nearby drive-in. I preached there to Rosie and Warren and the others who came in their cars.

The doctors said that Rosie would not live long, yet as the months went by she did not die. Another rainy winter came and I had to buy a new umbrella. Still Rosie did not die. Summer came and Rosie was doing exceptionally well. Another winter came and went. And I continued to stand in the open sky in the cold or rain, preaching to Rosie Gray and the others who gathered to worship in their cars.

After six years, God gave us the idea of selling our beautiful building. That's when I learned never to fall in love with a building, but to look beyond it. We bought ten acres of land and built a large building with open doors so that I could talk to people seated inside and talk to people outside in their cars at the same time. This church has always realized that although a person may be handicapped, he has great possibilities. "Out of your weakness shall come strength" (*see* Hebrews 11:34). If it had not been for Rosie Gray, this ministry would never have become what God intended it to be.

"You Made It!"

Let me share with you one of the most inspiring sights I've ever seen. It happened on the slopes of Squaw Valley at the National Handicapped Ski Championships. The skier was about eighteen, and blind. She was being led down the giant slalom. She made it through forty-four gates, until she was lined up straight with the finish line. Her guide behind her said, "Straight ahead, go for it!" She dug in, and was flying when she hit a rut. Her poles flew out of her hands. She fell flat on her stomach. She knew she'd have to get her body across the finish line or be disqualified. She looked beaten but she didn't stop. She reached out for her poles. When she couldn't find them, she started swimming over the snow straight ahead until she crossed the finish line.

The judge said, "You made it!" But she didn't hear him. She just kept swimming another five, ten, fifteen feet with all her heart.

The judge kept saying, "You made it! You can stop!" She still didn't hear. Finally it sunk in. "You made it!"

She stopped, flat on her belly, heard the applause, jumped to her feet, and danced for joy.

A Very Persistent Boy

I recently read the story of a little boy who went with his mother to the toy department of a store. A big sign read, "Children are not allowed to play with the toys or on the toys." Ignoring the sign, the little boy climbed on the hobbyhorse and started rocking back and forth. His mother said, "Come on, you've got to get down, you cannot play on that horse." He pushed her away and held on to the neck of the horse, even though his mother scolded and tugged at him. Finally, a clerk approached and said, "Sorry, but the sign says, 'No Children allowed on the toys.' But if your mother wants to buy it. . . ." The boy ignored him, so the clerk called the assistant manager, who grabbed the boy's arm and repeated, "Sonny, you're not allowed to play on that horse unless you buy it." The boy pushed him away, so the assistant manager called the manager. He also gave the youngster a lecture, explaining in very rational terms, "Sonny, if everybody came and played on these toys they would soon be broken and we could not sell them. We'd lose money. Now it's time to get off the horse." The little boy hung on tighter. Frustrated, the store manager called in the staff psychologist, who proceeded to go through all the various behavior-modification techniques and strategies to get the boy off the horse. But the kid wouldn't budge.

Finally, a tough, burly old man, who had been watching the entire scene, approached the frustrated motivators and said, "Let me talk to him." He went over and whispered something in the boy's ear. Immediately the boy jumped off the horse and said, "Okay, Mama, let's go home." Surprised, the mother asked, "What did that man say to you?" The youngster replied, "He told me, 'You get off the horse or I'll break every bone in your body!'"

Never Give Up

My friend Ralph Edwards once asked psychologist Joyce Brothers and myself to do some counseling on a television program called, "So You Think You've Got Troubles." On one program, we faced a woman who by her own admission was overweight. She said, "You may think my problem is my weight. I tried to lose weight. I went on diets, but kept gaining weight. Finally I decided that I am doomed to be fat. I decided to quit fighting it and just stay fat. But I also decided that I was going to enjoy being fat."

We asked her, "So what's your problem?" She said, "My

problem is that society is down on all fat people. I want to start a national organization to treat fat people nice. But I can't get people to take the idea seriously."

I can't condone the idea that anybody should ever give up the battle of their self-discipline. We didn't encourage her to accept her condition as final. The same may be true for you.

The Greatest Peacemakers I've Ever Met

I must tell you about the interesting time I had in Squaw Valley, California. Only a few weeks earlier I had lunch with the queen of England, and attended a dinner hosted by Bob Hope, but neither of those experiences compared with my visit to Squaw Valley. At that beautiful snow-covered mountain resort, I met the greatest collection of peacemakers I've ever met anywhere, including high-level meetings in Washington and around the world. The people I met in Squaw Valley topped them all.

They had gathered—hundreds of them—to compete in the Twelfth Annual National Handicapped Ski Championships. They had chosen for the site of their competition Squaw Valley, the 1960 home of the International Olympics.

I had carefully planned my week to include a trip to the Handicapped Nationals because my daughter Carol was skiing in them. As you may recall, Carol lost a leg in a motorcycle accident some years ago. When she became acquainted with the handicapped ski program, she decided to become a skier. She's been training hard for each of the twelve regional contests in America. All contestants must qualify in the Regionals before they can compete in the Nationals.

My heart was in my throat because I had never seen Carol ski before. She was scheduled to ski her first race on Thursday. I was to speak in Louisville on Wednesday, lecturing to the Christian theologians at the Southern Baptist Convention. My flight was to get me from Kentucky to Squaw Valley in time for the first race on Thursday. However, when the weatherman announced a blizzard was on its way, the first race was moved up to Wednesday. I missed it. I was terribly disappointed because that was her best race. She won the gold medal, first prize in the junior division in the downhill. I am very proud of her.

I missed that race, but on Friday the second races were to happen. My wife and I were there for those. Never had we seen so many one-legged people in one place. There were the triple amputees, with no legs and one arm missing. There were races for the blind—even a sightless race in the giant slalom.

The course is as long as the one that Olympians ski. They show no favoritism to the handicapped. There are forty-seven gates through which they have to maneuver coming down that mile-long, steep hill.

The blind were the first to ski. I'd never seen that before. They ski, followed or led down by a sighted person, who shouts directions, such as, "Turn to the right. Now to the left. Straight ahead. Quick, quick, to the right!" This is the way they ski and race. It's an amazing sight.

Then there are the three-trackers. Carol is a three-tracker. The three-trackers ski without a prosthesis, with a ski on their one good leg. They are aided by outriggers—poles with mini-skis on them.

In the first three-tracker race, which we missed, Carol related to us, "A funny thing happened. When the one-legged men skiers were coming down, one of the guys fell, and his leg became detached, not from the ski but from his knee, so that the leg and the ski came all the way down the hill and crossed the finish line! The judges didn't know whether they should award the leg or the body up on the hill!" These people have a fantastic sense of humor.

The athletes I met at Squaw Valley have made peace with themselves and with God. I'm talking about people who have lost legs, arms, sight, or mobility. They might have become bitter and angry at the world, but they didn't. They are at peace with themselves. They look in the mirror, they see what they are, and they've accepted it. They're not blaming God or anybody else. They are not fixing the blame, they're fixing the problem.

Snatched From Destruction

I was born and raised in an Iowa family where we always had bread with lots of butter. There was always an abundance of pie and desserts. Consequently, I was a fat butterball when I was a child. I had to struggle with my weight problem all my life. I tried diets. I counted calories. I still do. But the weight accumulated through the years. Finally I decided that I would eat only lean meats, vegetables, and fresh fruit for dessert.

One night I was taken out to dinner. The bread was passed. My host said, "This is fantastic. Feel it." I felt it—it was soft and warm. The fellow next to me was already spreading the butter, which was melting into the warm, fragrant bread. My host continued to tempt me. He said, "You must try the steak with the bearnaise sauce." I followed his advice. When it was time for dessert, I was feeling a little guilty. I was coaxed again, this time with, "They make the best pie here. It has a chocolate crust. You can't pass it by. Go on a diet tomorrow." I took the pie.

When I walked out of there, I calculated that I'd had three thousand calories. That night I went to bed filled with guilt and remorse. I woke up at two or three in the morning. I felt a total sense of futility because frankly, it was one time when possibility thinking totally failed me. I could build churches, towers, and a cathedral. I could write books, but I could not get rid of my fat. I could raise millions of dollars for God's work, but I couldn't turn my back on a piece of chocolate pie.

I remember praying out one simple prayer: "Dear Jesus, I don't know if You're dead or alive. I don't know if You're even real. I have believed it and I have preached it, but I couldn't prove it by my weight control. If You're there, can You help me?"

I was poor in spirit. I admitted my lack. I asked Him, and instantaneously, in my mind I saw the old Floyd River in Iowa. It was flooded way up to the grassy slopes. There in the middle of the stream was a great, gallant, strong, uprooted tree being carried away by the current. My body was that tree. The sloping hillside where the water lapped appeared harmless. It didn't look wild and it didn't look rough. It was safe. That was what butter, ice cream, and cake were for me. I was being destroyed by the seemingly harmless. Instantaneously, I heard the message. It was in the past perfect tense: *I have snatched you from destruction.*

I knew then that I had been liberated from subconscious forces that kept me addicted to sweets. I had an internal transformation. I still have my little ups and downs but never have reverted to what I was.

You have a problem. Admit it. There are people who would love to help you, starting with Jesus Christ.

A Successful Bean

I received a letter from a friend, Ansley Mueller, who lives in Pleasant Plains, Ohio. He sent me a little plastic case with a seed in it. There's a story behind it. You know, for years I've been teaching the principle "Any fool can count the seeds in an apple. Only God can count all the apples in one seed." Well, Ansley Mueller had been listening to this principle and one day he gave me the little seed with this true story. He said:

It was 1977, Dr. Schuller, and I lost half my crop. It was a bad, bad year. It was so wet, I couldn't get half of it harvested and it didn't develop. So, at the end of the year, in October, I would walk through the fields and try to pick up a bushel here and a piece there. Then, I saw standing by itself a most extraordinary, unusual looking soybean plant. I walked over and I was shocked by its size and its good looks. I went and carefully picked off the pods. There were 202 pods and I opened them and counted out 503 soybeans. I took them home. I kept them in a pan all winter and they dried out. The next spring they just seemed special to me. In 1978 I took those 503 soybeans and I planted them in a little plot behind my house and when October came I harvested thirty-two pounds! Thirty-two pounds! I dried them out in the winter and in 1979 I took those thirty-two pounds and I planted them on one acre and when October came, I harvested. I had 2,409 pounds and I planted them on sixty-eight acres, which was all the land I had available. In October, just a year ago, I harvested twenty-one hundred bushels and cashed it out for fifteen thousand dollars! Now, Dr. Schuller, one plant, four years later, fifteen thousand dollars. Not too bad, is it? So, Dr. Schuller, here's your bean. Good luck!

A Close Call

Not long ago, my wife and I were in Washington. Our return flight from Washington hit a squall. They kept us on the runway for forty minutes as a hurricane wind buffeted the plane. When we landed in Dallas, we had missed our connecting flight to California. It was crucial that I return to California in time to give the Sunday message.

As we landed in Dallas, we knew we'd missed our flight, but one of the attendants said, "There is a flight leaving for San Diego a few minutes after we land. Maybe you can get on it."

So just as soon as the plane landed, they buzzed us over on an electric cart. My wife and I weren't the only ones who had missed the flight—there were three others who were with us as they raced us to the boarding gate. But before we got halfway down there, we met others coming back. They said, "We've missed it! It's gone!"

The amazing thing is that I did not believe them. I practiced what I preached. I decided not to surrender to the first negative thought that came. Consequently, we didn't give up and we didn't turn back. Instead, we went on ahead. Sure enough, the accordian canvas had been folded back, leaving a great gap from the gate to the airplane. We had apparently missed the plane. Or had we? It was still there. It wasn't in the air. And anything's possible, right?

What would you have done if it had been you? Well, here's what I did: I walked to the edge and, holding on to the accordian canvas, I caught the pilot's attention. I called, "Hey!" He merely waved good-bye.

I said, "Open the door!"

He smiled again, then he saluted me. Just as I was beginning to think that it might be a good idea to try getting a train to California, a miracle happened. You talk about the Red Sea parting for Moses? Well, let me tell you, when the door of the airplane slowly and grandly opened, it was just as dramatic. The ground crew rolled the accordian back, my wife and I got on the plane, and so did three other people. The airlines made money on it. I think everybody was happy.

Robert Picking

I have a friend whom I met for the first time a few years ago when he was in his mid-nineties. At the time, he worked every day. He is Robert Picking, president of the Picking Company. His grandfather founded the company, his father propagated it, and the grandson is running the company today. The company was founded in 1874 in Cyrus, Ohio, and was called D. Picking and Company. It is the last of the old copper shops in America still making their original products primarily by hand.

I was thrilled to receive one of their products recently as a special gift from Bob Picking. It is a beautiful little shovel made out of solid copper. I treasure it not so much for what it is but for the labor and creativity that it represents. It was made by Bob Picking himself.

He was at work one day, as he is every day, when he noticed some cast-off pieces of copper piled in the trash. They weren't big enough for a skillet or a pot, and they weren't big enough for a kettle. Bob asked the workers what would happen to the odd-sized pieces of copper. They reported that it was waste, and that it would be melted down and disposed of. He said, "Nothing should be wasted. Nothing."

To prove his point he picked up one small piece and shaped it to form the scoop part of a small shovel. Then he took a long, narrow piece and rolled it to make a handle. He soldered the two pieces together into a beautiful work of art, and then he autographed it, "Robert Picking," and gave it to me. He never misses a day's work, and he never stops creating. Do you know how old he is now? He is 101 years old.

EXTRAORDINARY
VALUES

"Look for the Stars"

There was a woman who moved to the desert with her husband and found that life there was not happy at all. She wrote to her mother, saying, "I'm going to leave my husband. I can't stand living in the California desert. It's awful. There is only desert sagebrush and Indians. They don't seem interested in me and I can't really relate to them." Her mother wrote back these two lines: "Two people sit behind prison bars. One sees mud, and one sees stars." She continued, "Honey, look for the stars." So the woman did. She decided to get interested in the Indians. She got interested in the desert flowers and the desert stones and it became the most enriching time of her life.

"I Cut the Coal!"

This story is dedicated to people who are not at the top of the ladder but are nevertheless making America hum. I'm dedicating it to farmers, truck drivers, waitresses, retail clerks, and people dealing with the public (who are sometimes unnecessarily difficult). Yes, I'm dedicating this story to the people who are on the bottom rung of the salary scales in this country—to the janitor, to the gardener, and to the dishwasher in the back of the kitchen. The power of the simple, common person! It was Abraham Lincoln who said, "God must love the common people, because He made so many of them."

During the Second World War, Winston Churchill, a man respected and admired, was going up and down his scarred country trying to marshal the moral will of the people to withstand the assault of the enemy. He visited troops and factories and then someone suggested that he call on the coal miners. "If you could just stop in one of the little coal-mining towns, Mr. Churchill," one man pleaded. "They feel that they are doing nothing for the war effort. They don't get their pictures in the paper and they never receive any credit."

So Winston Churchill went down to visit the hardworking coal miners. He gazed at the greasy faces of these tough miners as they gathered (shocked that Winston Churchill would come to talk to them!). And the words he spoke that October day will never be forgotten. Standing before them, he said, "We will be victorious! We will preserve our freedom. And years from now when our freedom is secure and peace reigns, your children and your children's children will come and they will say to you, 'What did you do to win our freedom in that great war?' And one will say, 'I marched with the Eighth Army!' Someone else will proudly say, 'I manned a submarine.' And another will say, 'I guided the ships that moved the troops and the supplies.' And still another will say, 'I doctored the wounds!' " Then he paused. The dirty-faced miners, with their caps pushed back, sat in silence and awe waiting for him to continue. "They will come to you," he shouted, "and you will say, with equal right and equal pride, 'I cut the coal! I cut the coal that fueled the ships that moved the supplies! That's what I did. I cut the coal!' "

The Most Valuable Possessions

I remember calling on a very rich woman who had suffered a great personal tragedy. She had vases from the Ming Dynasty; she had jewels and many other beautiful and valuable things. She greeted me and said, "Dr. Schuller, I once heard you say on television, 'Trouble never leaves you where it found you.' That is so true."

She said, "These things don't mean nearly as much to me now. Oh, I still love them. I'm not going to throw them away. But if there were a fire, I wouldn't take that Chinese vase as I would have before. Do you know what I'd take? The family pictures."

When tragedy hits, values change. The family becomes important—the husband, the wife, and the children. When your values change, your life changes.

I Believe in Success

I recall a dear friend I went to school with many years ago. He was a socialist. I am not of that same economic persuasion, so we often had friendly debates about the implications of the philosophy. Once, after talking some minutes, I finally said, "You keep saying that managing to make a profit is a sin, a social irresponsibility. I respect your opinion, but I view the situation a different way. I say to manage to obtain a profit is not wrong in and of itself. Profit is only wrong when handled in a socially irresponsible manner. To me, the great crime against society is to manage for a loss."

I believe in success—the alternative is failure. When you or I fail, we can be sure that someone down the road is missing an opportunity for employment because of that failure.

Stop and Smell the Roses

At Easter I am reminded of a time many years ago when I had a touch from Jesus Christ that was most meaningful. It was early in our church's history. We had started a drive-in, and then we got the dream of building a walk-in, drive-in church and turning it into a Garden of Eden with fountains and waters and flowers and birds and beautiful pieces of sculptured architecture. I presented the ideas to my small band of people, about three hundred members. Of the three hundred, almost half of them thought it was a crazy, wild, awful idea. The others thought it was fantastic. I was in the middle.

When you're a pastor of a congregation and it's split down the middle, with half of them totally enthusiastic and the others dead set against it, you have what's called a problem. This was my problem. And it got worse.

Unknown to me, a dissonant element in the church hired an assistant minister for one specific purpose: to meet with them privately and secretly to see how they could possibly have me fired. Meanwhile, I was saddled with an unavoidable commitment to the church board to give leadership to this church. I had a problem that had no apparent solution and which became a pressure that I couldn't run away from. My dream became a depression.

Thank God my major in undergraduate work was psychology. If it hadn't been for that, I don't know if I could have survived. But even then, in spite of my intellectual, rational knowledge of the emotional processes that were at work within me, I was unable to sort it out. I was so depressed that the will to die was stronger than the will to live.

About that time, *Life* magazine came out with a cover picture of the back of a minister's head and his robe. You couldn't see his face. But the headline read: "Why Protestant ministers are cracking up." I thought, *Oh boy, I'm next.*

That night I was unable to sleep. Hour after hour I tossed and turned. The sheets became hot. I began to perspire. Panic approached me. I thought *Schuller, you're cracking up.* As I became controlled by the fear that I was having a nervous breakdown, I desperately prayed a prayer more sincere than any prayer I'd ever prayed. I said, "Jesus Christ, are You dead or alive? I've been preaching it every Easter. But are You a myth? Are You a legend? Or are You really alive? Do You care?"

What happened next I shall never forget so long as I live, and even as I retell it now I feel shivers under my robe. I felt a finger go through the skull bone deep into my brain, like a surgeon's finger probing at flesh that has been anesthetized. I could feel that pressure but no pain. The finger went deep and it slowly withdrew, and as it did it took with it all anxiety, all depression, and all fear of failure. Peace flowed from the top of my head over my body. He touched me and made me whole. He was alive.

I knew then that He would not let me fail. I fell into the deepest sleep and awoke the next morning, walked out the door to go to my office, and stopped in my tracks, startled by the beautiful roses. I turned quickly and said to my wife, "Honey, the roses are blooming." She said, "Oh, Bob, they've been blooming for three months." They had been blooming, but I never saw them. I was totally unaware of them. My anxieties had paralyzed my perception of beauty around me.

Scale It Down

When we started in the drive-in theater, many years ago, I began to dream of a church of my own. My first dream was for a forty-acre plot on Katella Avenue. I was sure that we needed forty acres. And I was sure that Katella was the best location. However, when a forty-acre parcel on Katella became available, we couldn't afford it. I negotiated; I compromised. I decided that we actually needed only ten acres. That was all we bought. Later on, we added another ten acres; now we're up to twenty. Better half a loaf than none!

People who never change their minds are either perfect or stubborn. You're not perfect, you don't want to be stubborn, so be willing to occasionally change your mind. Scale down, if necessary.

Don't Exaggerate Your Problems

Recently I visited Mainland China. My uncle and I went inland from Amoy to Changchun with the official guides of the Communist regime. While in Changchun we went to church and returned to our hotel for lunch. As I was about to go out for a little stroll, I was told I could not leave the hotel. I was under virtual house arrest for four hours!

Now I've been in the Soviet Union three times and this was my third trip to the People's Republic. But this was the first time in all my international travels that I was confined to my hotel without my approval.

The People's Republic guide, a lovely, young girl, tried to explain. She said, "You don't understand, Dr. Schuller." To which I replied, "I do understand. I understand what freedom is—you don't. If you came to the United States of America you could travel freely from state to state. There you don't need papers to go from city to city."

See your problems in their proper perspective. Don't exaggerate. You're still in the United States of America, and you can go anywhere you choose.

Commitment for Energy

Not long ago I read in the newspaper about the newest fads in the Los Angeles area. It detailed what was "in" and what was "out." Designer jeans are now out, and old Levis are in. Certain restaurants are now out, and other ones are in. Tennis is out, and racquetball is also going out. Golf is coming back in. (Not that golf impresses me, though. I used to play golf until I tried applying my principles of possibility thinking to it. When it threatened my religion, I gave up.) Anyway, the article surveyed the cities and life-styles of America. One exciting thing it pointed out is that living together before marriage is going out, and marriage is coming back in. In other words, commitment is in.

Answer this question: What commitment would you make this morning if you knew it could not fail? Maybe it is marriage. Are you willing to make the plunge of commitment? If you are, here's what will happen. Commitment will produce energy. Energy will produce enthusiasm. Enthusiasm will produce a whole new way of living.

Don't Miss the Sunset

An artist was teaching his students how to paint. On a special occasion, he took them on an all-night trip to a hill because the sunsets were so beautiful there. They were all painting the sunset. Just as the colors broke (purples and reds and pinks and oranges and yellows, golds, greens), the teacher walked around the students and he noticed that one student was very busy painting the shingles on the barn in the valley under the sunset. There he was, tediously painting the shingles!

The teacher told him to paint the sunset and forget the shingles. "If you don't forget the shingles, the sunset will be gone and you'll have missed it," the teacher said.

What's the point? The point is, don't miss the positive that's passing. You can get so locked up on the shingles that you miss the sunset. You can concentrate so much on the negatives that you don't notice the positives.

Do as Lincoln Did

At the height of the Civil War, Lincoln and his secretary of war visited the battlefield home of General George McClellan. They waited in the parlor of McClellan's home for the general to return from the front. Finally the door opened and in walked the general. He saw the president and the secretary of war but never acknowledged them. Instead he walked by them and on up the stairs to his room. They assumed he would be down very soon, so they continued to wait. When he did not appear they sent the maid to inquire. She returned and said, "I'm sorry, Mr. President, but the general asked me to tell you that he is tired and has gone to bed."

The secretary of war was shocked and said, "Mr. President, that's unacceptable. You must relieve him of command." Lincoln thought about it for a minute, then said, "No, I will not relieve him; that man wins battles. I would hold his horse and wash the dirt from his boots if he could shorten this bloodshed by one hour."

A Value Problem

A recent issue of *Time* magazine had on its cover a face of someone distorted in agony. The headline read, "Anxiety; How Are We Going to Deal With It?" As I keep up my studies in psychology and human behavior I can tell you that boredom, depression, and anxiety, as well as other emotional and mental problems, are epidemic in America. The interesting phenomenon is that they are no longer restricted to the poverty pockets of our country. They are also rampant among the affluent. What this means is that your depression or your anxiety is not necessarily related to your state of employment or unemployment. The depression and anxiety epidemic is not a money problem. It is a value problem.

We don't need money. We need to get a dream, a desire for something we'd die for. Some of you are teenagers and some of you are in college. Some of you have been out of college for years, yet you still don't know what you really want to do with the one life you have to live.

The World Is Throbbing With Life

I will always remember Asa Skinner. He was a member of my first church in Chicago, Illinois. He was a fine executive who was always active. He underwent brain surgery for a tumor, and I wondered how he'd be able to tolerate the long recovery period at home. I called on him shortly after he was discharged from the hospital. His wife met me at the door. I said, "How is Asa doing?" She replied, "Oh, very good." I asked, "How are his spirits?" She answered, "They're fantastic. Come on, you can see why."

I found him in his tiny backyard, sitting in a chair with his bathrobe on and his head bandaged in white. His wife told me he was studying. As I approached him I noticed that he was looking at the ground through binoculars. When he saw me, he said, "Oh, Dr. Schuller, look at them!" He was watching the ants build a home and transport material. He said, "I've been noticing the wasps. Look at the nest they built." Then he pointed in the far distance where there was a tree. He said, "See, in that tree a robin is building a nest."

The ants, the wasps, the robin. He said, "Dr. Schuller, this world is throbbing with life and all of life is so beautiful; it's a pity that a single insect has to die."

Nothing Is Ordinary

William Wolcott, the great English artist, came to New York City in 1924 to record his impression of that skyscraper city. After a week of beginning to feel it, one morning he found himself in the architectural office of a colleague for whom he'd worked years before in England. And now suddenly the urge and surge to sketch came over him. And he quickly said to his colleague, "Please, I need some paper." And seeing some paper on a desk, he said, "May I have that?" The architectural colleague said, "That's not sketching paper, Mr. Wolcott. That's just ordinary wrapping paper." Wolcott, not wanting to lose the inspiration, reached out and said, "Nothing is ordinary if you know how to use it." And he took that drawing paper and made two sketches. One sold for one thousand dollars and the other sold for five hundred dollars. The principle: Nothing is ordinary if you know how to use it.

Not Necessarily Lazy

You know, Henry Ford once hired an efficiency expert to go through his plant. He said, "Try to find nonproductive people, tell me who they are, and I will fire them." The man returned and reported that he definitely found such a person. "Every time I walk by his door," he said, "he is sitting with his feet propped up on his desk. When I go in, he stands, shakes hands, we exchange a few words, and when I leave he props his feet up on his desk again. The man never does a thing." When Henry Ford learned the name of the man he said, "Well, I can't fire him—I pay him to do that. I pay him to do nothing but think."

You need one day in seven when you can have an experience in a church to do nothing but think. Get another shot of rejoicing and recharging and renewal power, and your dreams and your ideals will be resurrected.

Coming or Going?

I remember a time when we were rushing to catch a hydrofoil. It was in Naples, Italy, where the hydrofoil runs to the island of Capri. There is also a ferry that runs back and forth. One man came running alongside the pier. He took a running leap, jumped three feet, and landed on the moving ferry. He breathlessly exclaimed, "Wow, I made it!"

The deckhand said, "What's your hurry? We'd have been along the pier in another minute." Some people don't know whether they're coming or going.

"If You Don't Know . . ."

I have a favorite story of a wise professor who was so learned and had so many credentials that he could teach whatever he chose. He could teach biology, history, or astronomy. One day he decided to motivate one of his young students by planning an all-day canoe trip in the wilderness. He hoped to show him how education is meaningful in human existence.

The day was just dawning when the student and the old professor started out in their canoe. As they drifted downriver, a leaf fell into the quiet water and the professor picked it up and handed it to the student. "Now tell me, do you understand the leaf?" The boy answered, "No." The wise old man said, "See, my son, if you do not learn biology, you will miss out on twenty percent of life's potential joy."

As the canoe rounded a bend, rocks that hovered above the water's edge revealed markings of Indians from many years ago. The old professor said, "See those markings? Do you know what Indians made those markings, and how they lived?" The boy said, "I don't know." "My son," said the professor, "If you do not learn history, you'll miss out on another twenty percent of life's enjoyment."

As they maneuvered through the shallow waters, the old man's wrinkled hand reached down and scooped up some pebbles. He handed the stones to the boy and asked, "Of what geological period is this rock?" The boy said, "I don't know, what kind of rock is it?" The professor said, "If you don't know geology, you're missing out on another twenty percent of life." Shortly after, darkness fell, and the first star came out. The old man pointed to a constellation and asked, "What star is that?" The boy again said, "I don't know."

"My son," the professor said, "if you do not understand biology and history and astronomy, you are missing out on sixty percent of life. You will only be living life on a very shallow level." Suddenly they heard a loud roar and realized their canoe was rapidly being carried along by the swift current. The roar ahead of them grew louder and the student asked, "Professor, do you know how to swim?" The old man said, "No." As the boy dove into the river and swam to shore he yelled back, "Then you're missing out on one hundred percent of life!"

You Can't Kid Nature

As many of you know, I was born on an Iowa farm. Adjoining my family's farm was a river, which thrilled me because I loved to fish. I remember one time when a city kid came to visit the neighbors across the road for a few weeks. The city kid was our neighbor's nephew. His uncle had welcomed him but warned that he would have to help out with the work.

One day Uncle Harry gave his nephew a can of beans to plant. He explained, "Just dig a little hole, put in a couple of beans, and step it down. Do it all the way along the fence, 'til you get to the end."

Unaware of the task that had been assigned to this city lad, I invited him to join me fishing.

He replied, "Uncle Harry said I have to plant these beans. He said I have to dig a little hole, put in three beans, and step it down."

I said, "Oh, that's too bad. I wish you could go fishing with me. Ever been fishing?"

"No. I'd like to go fishing with you, but I've got to finish these beans." From the looks of the full can it appeared that he'd just started. Suddenly, directly in front of him was a stump. "Uncle Harry will never know," he said, as he dug a hole, dumped in all the beans, and covered them with dirt. He turned away from his task and said, "Let's go fishing!"

We had a grand time. We caught a good number of fish. Coming home with bullheads, we ran into Uncle Harry.

He said, "I see you've been fishin'. Did you get all the beans planted?"

His nephew said, "Sure did, Uncle Harry."

"That's great. Glad to hear it. And you still had time to fish?"

"M-m-m, yeah."

"I'm surprised you were able to plant them so quickly."

He answered, "I work fast."

Uncle Harry seemed to accept his word for it. Soon it was time for the boy to return home. Months passed. The summer was drawing to a close. The city kid returned for a last visit before school started.

Uncle Harry said to him, "Hey, would you like to see those beans you planted?" They walked out behind the farmhouse. There was a neat row of beans for about fifty feet. Suddenly there was a stump of a tree covered with uncontrolled vines.

The lesson is this: You can't kid nature and you can't play with God. You can't avoid principles and you can't tamper with natural laws. This is a natural law: If you treat people nicely, they'll treat you nicely. It is the law of proportionate return, and there's no way of getting around it.

Real Quality

I recently read a fascinating story by John Dart in the *Los Angeles Times*. In it, he described how Johann Gutenberg, who died in 1468, took with him his publishing secrets. The Gutenberg Bible, unlike all other known print on paper, still has jet-black ink after five hundred years. There is no seepage through the paper and the edges of letters are perfectly sharp. Twenty-four people, headed by Dr. Schwab and Dr. Cahill of the University of California at Davis, have been using the cyclotron to find the secret of Gutenberg's ink. They have finally discovered that Gutenberg used unusually high lead and copper content. In essence, the ink he used was closer to paint than it was to ink.

Gutenberg's secret? No frills. He went for real quality. If you want to succeed in life, don't go for cheap thrills.

EXTRAORDINARY
GENEROSITY

God Protected Us

There's a man alive today enjoying life and health who probably would have died from lung cancer if he hadn't listened to one of my messages and made a decision. He and his wife left church that morning and decided they were going to tithe. They looked at the money they had left and they said, "There's no way we can get by." But then he looked at his wife, and she looked at him and said, "If we tithe, the only way we can get by is if we cut something out of our life that we're spending money on now." He replied, "But there's nothing we're spending money on that we can cut out." She said, "Unless we quit smoking."

It was true, if they quit smoking, then they could afford it. He said, "I guess it's not right to take God's money and buy our tobacco." They quit smoking and he later shared with me, "I believe that God has prospered me by tithing, and He has probably protected both my wife and me from lung cancer."

A Gift From the Heart

Recently, I donated my Good Shepherd medallion to our charity auction. Prior to the event, I had announced on television my plan to make this donation. A lady in New York City, who has watched the "Hour of Power" faithfully, heard what was going to happen and decided she would buy the medallion regardless of the cost. She flew to California to attend the auction and was prepared to bid any amount.

The medallion was worth only one thousand dollars, but she bought it for sixty-four hundred dollars. All of the money went to our mission project. The day after the auction she stopped to see me before her return to New York. Enthusiastically she said, "Dr. Schuller, the real reason I bought the medallion was I felt you should always have it." Then she gave me back my medallion as a gift!

Surrender to Compromise

Albert Schweitzer built a hospital in the African jungle. One day he asked one of the natives to carry some wood. The native, who had been learning to read and write, replied, "I'd like to, sir, but it's beneath my dignity. I am a scholar, an intellectual."

Albert Schweitzer chuckled and said, "I've always wanted to be an intellectual, too, but I never quite made it, so I'll carry the wood!" And he went out and carried the wood.

A Beautiful Gift

I'll never forget the young girl who came to me. She was pregnant, and she could not marry the man. She wanted to know whether she should get an abortion or not.

I said to her, "Look, I can't make your decision for you. I can, however, share with you a principle that will help you make the right choice. I want you to think of one thing— there is a negative and positive solution—and then let your conscience be your guide."

It was many months later when I next saw her. She looked so happy. She said, "I just gave a beautiful gift to a beautiful couple."

I asked, "What gift did you give?"

She said, "A baby. They told me that my baby was an answer to prayer." Then she added this: "Dr. Schuller, you often say that the bottom line in giving is being unselfish. Giving is living, and I'll always know that I gave the world something beautiful."

The Best That I Had

Some years ago there was a play called *Eagerheart*. It was the story of a beautiful, eager, young peasant girl named Eagerheart, who lived in a simple little country hut. The news reached the town and the surrounding farming huts that the king of England would be coming through the territory. That meant that he could knock on any door and hospitality would be extended to him.

Eagerheart couldn't wait for the day when the king was expected to pass through town. She cleaned her little hut, swept the floor, and pressed the curtains. Everything was clean, fresh, and sweet-smelling.

Just as she was ready to rush to the village, so she wouldn't miss him, another peasant woman with a shawl over her head and a baby in her arms, came to her door and said, "I am tired from a long journey. May I come in for rest and water?"

Eagerheart said, "I must go to the village to meet the king, who is coming to town. But, yes, you may come in. You may rest, you may have water. But I can't stay. Good-bye." With that, she rushed off to the village.

As she made her way to the village, she met three Oriental men, bearing what looked like expensive gifts. They asked her directions to the countryside and she pointed them down the path that she'd just taken. She wondered what those strange, rich-looking men would be doing near her place. One of the men, noticing the question in her eyes, said, "We are astrologers. We read the stars and the stars tell us a king is coming."

Eagerheart said, "I know, that's why I'm going to the village."

They said, "But our stars tell us we can find him in the country."

She did not challenge them but thought that was strange. She kept going until she got to the village. Suddenly she saw many villagers streaming out of the town. She asked one, "Where are you going?" He replied, "The king is coming, and the word is that he's out in the country."

So Eagerheart followed the crowd, and lo and behold, the parade led to her own little hut. She said, "He can't be in there, that is my place!" But she ran up and opened the door and there was the old woman whose head was covered with a shawl, the woman who carried a simple, little child, whom she had admitted to her home so casually and left when she went to the village. Now the woman stood, the shawl was removed, and Eagerheart recognized the old woman as the queen mother of England and the baby as the new king. Eagerheart dropped to her knees, and she said, "Oh, had I stayed home, I could have spent the time alone with him!" But then she added, "At least I gave him the best that I had."

Give Someone a Lift

There is a story of a man who had a dream one night. He dreamed that he died and found himself in a large room. In the room there was a huge banquet table filled with all sorts of delicious food. Around the banquet table were people seated on chairs. They were obviously hungry. But the chairs were five feet from the edge of the table and the people apparently could not get out of the chairs. Furthermore, their arms were not long enough to reach the food on the table.

In the dream there was a solitary large spoon, five feet long. Everyone was fighting, quarreling, and pushing each other, trying to grab hold of the spoon. The man reached out, picked up some food, and turned it to feed himself, only to find that the spoon was so long that as he held it out he could not touch his mouth. The food fell off.

Immediately, someone else grabbed the spoon. That person reached far enough to pick up the food, but could not feed himself. The handle was too long.

In his dream, the man who was observing it all said to his guide, "This is hell; to have food and not be able to eat it." The guide replied, "Where do you think you are? This is hell. But this is not your place. Come with me."

And they went into another room. In this room there also was a long table, filled with food, exactly as in the other room. Everyone was seated in chairs, and for some reason they, too, seemed unable to get out of their chairs.

Like the others, they were unable to reach the food on the table. Yet they had a satisfied, pleasant look on their faces. Only then did the visitor see the reason. For exactly as before, there was only one spoon. It, too, had a handle five feet long. Yet no one was fighting for it. In fact, one man who held the handle reached out, picked up food, and put it into the mouth of someone else who ate and was satisfied.

That person then took the spoon by the handle, reached for the food from the table, and put it back to the mouth of the man who first gave him something to eat. And the guide said, "This is heaven."

If you want to be fed, you have to feed someone else. If you want happiness, you have to forget about your own happiness and look for someone who needs the lift that only you can give.

Caring Is Carrying

In the villages in the Bahamas today, they still do something that has been a tradition for years.

Before I tell you what it is, let me tell you about the kind of family I came from. In our little Dutch ethnic community in Iowa, it was a custom that if somebody became ill, my mother would bake a pie, or cookies, or a loaf of bread, and take it to the neighbor. It was the natural thing to do when someone was sick. But I never before heard of what they do in the Bahamas. You go to the villages in the Bahamas and about suppertime everybody cooks their food. As you walk down the street you can smell the delicious fragrances in the air. Everybody seems to eat about the same time, but before they sit down in their home to eat, the doors open and the people walk out of their front doors with plates. They have made more than an abundance of food. So they take a plate of home-baked food and carry it across the street to share with a neighbor. Soon another neighbor comes to their house and shares his food.

It reminds me of the times when my wife and I go out for dinner and I order a different entrée than she does. If mine is very good, I want her to share my taste of joy. So I say, "Would you like to taste my entrée?" And she says, "Yes." And I cut a piece and share it with her. And she gives me a portion of hers. Caring is carrying. It's a law of life.

A Touching Scene

I've been to many of the world's most beautiful Christmas pageants, including the Glory of Christmas that is held every year in the Crystal Cathedral. But nothing has touched me more than the scene in the Christmas pageant that was held in a little country school in Iowa.

The star of that pageant was a young fellow named Howard who was big and rather awkward. He was given the role of the Innkeeper. He was so excited that he rehearsed his one line until he could say it perfectly. His line was, "There's no room in my inn." When Mary and Joseph came to him on stage, he was to face them gruffly and say, "There is no room in my inn."

When the pageant finally took place, on opening night, Joseph came with Mary, who was almost stumbling, tired, in distress. They came up to little Howard, who was playing the role of Innkeeper, and Joseph said, "I'm looking for a room for my wife." And Howard, who had memorized his lines, suddenly saw Mary, and felt terrible. A tear welled up in his eye, rolled down his cheek, and he said, "Oh, come on in, you can have my room!"

Give Something Back

How do you handle debt? That's the big question. I like George Kennedy's attitude. This esteemed actor not too long ago said to me, "Every time my wife, Joan, and I sit down to a meal, we always begin with the same little prayer. We look at the food we're about to consume and we say, 'Oh, Lord, help us to give something back.' " What a fantastic prayer! We all should learn how to give. Most of us don't know how, you know.

Take, for example, the average college alumnus. Most alumni give very, very little to their institutions, even though they're making money based on their education. Here's why: They think they don't owe any more to their school. They've paid their tuition, which was high, so they feel they've given back all that was expected. In reality, they haven't given a thing. They only paid their bill. Giving doesn't start until you've paid what you owe.

The Beautiful Hazel Wright

I have never met anyone whom I consider more beautiful than Hazel Wright. As my wife and I have come to know her, we have learned the secret of her beauty. What is it? She knows how to give. She's not selfish.

Selfish people are not pretty people. They are cautious, conservative, security-conscious people who are dominated by worry and fear. On the other hand, giving people are dominated by joy, love, faith, and hope. It's really true. The measure with which you give will be reflected in your personality.

Many years ago Hazel's husband began to prosper in his enterprises. He would buy her little gifts. She said to him one day, "I don't need things. I thank you for your love—that's enough for me." So Hazel's husband, rather than buying her jewelry or other pretty things, gave his wife some stock in the company. The stock accumulated because she never spent it on herself.

Hazel never was a mother. She remained childless until she saw great institutions and organizations that were threatened. Because she is a caring, compassionate woman, she decided to adopt and support these floundering projects. Then when her husband died, she decided to keep his love alive to some degree by continuing to give whatever she could to those who really needed it.

As a result, if you're ever in Palm Springs at the Eisenhower Memorial Hospital, you will see three large buildings. One carries the name The Wright Building. Hazel Wright had that building constructed for the sick and the suffering.

A Way of Saying Thanks

I recently called Kathy Gill. Kathy is one of our staff people. She's in Seattle undergoing a bone marrow transplant because it's the only thing that can save her life. What powerful faith! She said, "Oh, it's wonderful just to look outdoors and see the sun shining." Kathy is a young mother, not more than thirty years old. She is so grateful just to be alive. *Alive.* If you are given the gift of life, my friend, and the gift of health, and if you're not living under a death sentence right now, you should be so grateful to God. A tenth is almost nothing to give as a way of saying thanks.

Go for the Touchdown

One day years ago when I was at Western Theological Seminary, a guest lecturer came and spoke, of all things, on money. He said, "Students, you will soon be going out as pastors of churches. If you do a good job you're going to need money. If you fail, you won't need anything. But if you succeed, you're going to need money and a lot of it.

"Then, how can the church get the money to do the job? The Bible has an answer: God's way is to convince people to give one-tenth of their income back to God. It's called tithing. In Malachi 3, the Lord says, 'Bring your whole tithe into my storehouse and prove me and see if I will not open the windows and pour out such a blessing there will not be room enough to receive it' " (*see* verse 10).

I raised my hand and said, "I am a seminary student earning twenty dollars a week cleaning toilets. Are you telling me that I'm supposed to give ten percent, or two dollars, in the offering plate each Sunday?"

He said, "Yes."

I said, "I don't think I can afford that."

He replied, "You can't afford not to. If you trust God, He will give you the wisdom to make your eighteen dollars go further than the twenty dollars would." That was the toughest decision I ever made. But at the close of his lecture, he said, "I think we all ought to pray about this."

Then he did something that I had never seen before. Normally, I would have found it repulsive and manipulative. But, in his closing prayer, he said, "God, I sense that somebody here needs to believe what You have promised us in the Bible. I pray that this person will make a decision now to practice tithing all his life. If you want to make such a decision, will you now raise your hand?"

I found my hand going up. When I had it in the air, I thought, *Oh, dear, what have I done? Lord, have I promised You that I'll give You 10 percent?*

I was absolutely astounded that I'd done such a thing, because I'd had it tough, financially. My family had just lost everything in a tornado. Then a fire burned my dormitory. I had to buy new clothes. I don't think anybody was poorer than I was. Yet, I had just promised God I would give Him 10 percent of all I had.

However, it was the greatest decision I ever made in my life, because I heard a little voice deep down that said, *Schuller, if you don't have enough faith to grab that idea from God, you won't have enough faith to grab hold of some of the bigger ideas He wants to throw your way. If you can't catch a short pass, how do you think you can jump and catch the big one and go for the touchdown?*

Well, I went for it, and six years later I received the call to begin a church from scratch. My denomination had promised me a salary of $375 a month for six months. After that, I was on my own. I also received a gift of $400 from the little church that I'd served in Chicago.

On our way to California, my wife and I stopped and saw a friend who was in the music business in Sioux City, Iowa. I said, "I'm going to California to start a new church. I don't have any members yet. I don't own any property, but I do have four hundred dollars in my pocket. I have a wife who is an organist. I'd like to buy an organ. Can you sell me an organ?"

He replied, "I'll sell you this Kahn electric organ for eighteen hundred dollars. I'll take your four hundred dollars as a down payment. The balance will be thirty-six dollars a month for thirty-six months."

I said, "It's a deal." Since I was a tither, I knew that for six months I would be getting $375 a month. Ten percent of $375 is $37 a month. Consequently I knew I could make the monthly payments on the organ. If I hadn't been a tither, I wouldn't have purchased the organ.

That was just the first step. If I hadn't had enough faith to try tithing, I would never have had the nerve to grab hold of all the bigger ideas that God was getting ready to send my way.

In Appreciation

Recently in Florida, a husband and a wife, both about sixty-two years of age, took my hand and with tears in their eyes, told me their story.

They said, "Dr. Schuller, we want to give all our property in our will to your ministry."

I said, "Wait a minute. Thank you, but you know, you must remember your children first."

They said they had no children.

I said, "But you must have dear friends who have helped you."

They said, "We have no friends dearer than you. Eight years ago we had decided to end our lives together. We researched it. We had scientifically planned how we were going to kill ourselves in a suicide pact. And the day that we planned to do it, we turned the television set on to find out how the weather would be affecting our plans. We were flipping the dial and we saw you. All we saw was a smile. And it stopped us cold. And then you told us about Jesus, that He was alive." By this time they were weeping openly. They said, "Reverend Schuller, that was eight years ago. Everything is wonderful now."

A Unique Ministry

Not long ago I received a letter from a charter member of our church, Clara Landrus. She wrote me about her mother, Katherine Grant, who just recently passed away at the age of ninety-three. Mrs. Grant lived as a shut-in for the past eight years up in the small town of Clarkston, Washington. According to Clara, her mother began every Sunday morning with the "Hour of Power." October 25 was her last Sunday with this television ministry, for on November 1 she went to be with Jesus, where there is no sunset and no dawning.

As a shut-in, Mrs. Grant had a unique ministry. She had people come and visit her, and when they did, she would give them a lift. Clara's mother kept a diary and recorded her daily events. In the past ten months, Mrs. Grant had a total of 357 visits by 81 different people. Those who visited her left feeling better. One person summed it up to Clara: "Your mother put a bloom on so many days for so many people."

EXTRAORDINARY FAITH

When Proof Is Possible
Faith Is Impossible

One summer I was in Tokyo for an evangelism event. I was to speak to a few thousand Japanese people who claimed to have no faith at all. Before I talked to them, I visited with several of them at great length, trying to understand where they were coming from.

I asked them, "What would you call yourselves?"

They replied almost unanimously, "We are atheists."

I said, "Why are you atheists?"

The combined answer was, "We are very scientific. We do not believe in something that cannot be proven."

My answer to them came from my subconscious. I heard myself say it before I thought it, therefore, I know it came from God. The answer was, "That's a contradiction, for the truth is, when proof is possible, faith is impossible."

If you know all of the answers, you don't need any faith. If you have absolute conclusive proof of any position, it requires no trust to move forward.

Faith is a behavioral human response when you're challenged to make a choice and you cannot be certain of either of the options. That's what faith is.

So then the question arises, "If there is a God, why didn't He prove it to us?" The answer is simple: If He proved Himself to you (and it would be easy for Him to prove Himself) you could never be a believer—you would simply be a follower.

Moses: A Great Possibility Thinker

Moses was a great possibility thinker. When he was urged to take the children of Israel out of Egypt, he left, even though he had no way of knowing how he would get those people across the Red Sea. If he had waited to leave until the solution to his problem was apparent to him, God would never have parted the waters.

At the heart of the meaning of faith is a very important principle: God never performs a miracle until you've committed yourself to something beyond your ability.

God's Biggest Job

As I left my house one day, I was enthusiastic about going to work. I rushed into the garage, threw my briefcase into the backseat, started the car, and backed out of the garage. But something didn't feel right. I jumped out of the car and discovered I had a flat tire. Have you ever had the experience of a slow leak? Or have you ever had the experience of a blowout? Have you ever had the experience of feeling self-confident, beginning to believe you were an attractive person made by God? Then someone gave you a rebuff or a rejection, and what happened? It was like a self-confidence blowout.

Maybe your work doesn't go well. You aren't receiving the recognition you deserve and you don't believe that people appreciate you. What is that? That's like a slow leak. And one day you wake up and the tire is flat. The self-confidence is gone.

God's biggest job is to keep you believing. He made you. He's planning your life. You're great! That's His biggest job—to keep your self-confidence up day after day.

Eternal Life

I recall the wife of a congressman from Orange County in California. She had two children, a son and a daughter. Both of them were killed when they were teenagers. Her husband also died at a fairly early age. She was completely alone. You know, it's easy to go to someone and say, "Don't look at what you have lost, look at what you've got left." But here was a case where she had no one left.

I said, "Where do you find comfort? What gives you the strength to keep going?"

She said, "I live in Long Beach. I used to go to the beach every day. Often I just sat there, numb. I could not think. I could not feel, but I could see. And I watched the waves as they built into a curl of foam as they washed up onto the sand and retreated. I did that, day after day, week after week, month after month, and year after year. One day, as I watched the waves curl, break, foam, and sweep across the sand, I was struck with a message from God. I heard a voice within me say, *There is nothing but eternal life.*"

And she said, "I knew where my son was. I knew where my daughter was, and where my husband was."

A Telegram for Humphrey

I remember sending a telegram to my friend Hubert Humphrey, before he went to the hospital for major surgery in New York City. I was in the music department when my secretary buzzed me and said Hubert Humphrey was on the phone. When I picked up the receiver he said, "Hello, Bob, I'm so glad I got hold of you. I'm going into major surgery in a few hours and I wanted to thank you for your inspiring telegram. My staff just brought in a large stack of telegrams and letters, neatly pressed and sorted. I was browsing through a few of them and guess whose was on top!"

I said, 'The president of the United States?" He laughingly said, "No, Bob, yours was! I have it before me now and I'm drawing so much strength from it." (The telegram read: "Dear Mr. Humphrey, God wanted me to send His Scripture to you. 'I have a plan for your life, it is a plan for good, not evil. It is a plan to give you a future with hope!' Jeremiah 29:11.")

Every person listening to me needs that inner strengthening that can only come from God, who is bigger than you or me! Now when heartache hits, difficulties block your path, or progress seems retarded and you wonder if you should pack up and quit—hang on! We will never know how many people failed because they gave up on faith. Don't ever quit!

Laguna Canyon

Many years ago, before the area was developed, a friend of mine from Orange County was riding through the hills of Laguna Canyon with another Orange County resident. They passed a large herd of cows grazing on a hillside. My friend Chuck said, "You know, John, I am worried about my cows. It's been a dry summer. I sure hope they get enough water to drink."

John looked at him and said, "I didn't know you owned these cows and that ranch. I thought it was Irvine property." Chuck said, "Oh, no, John, I own all those cows, I own all those hills, and I own this road. You know what, John? So do you. Every night I look down at all the twinkling lights in Laguna Beach, and I say, 'I own it all. I'm just glad I don't have to manage it!' " He said, "Sure. You know, John, it says in the Bible, 'The cattle and the fowl of the hills are mine.' God owns everything and we are His children. *We* own it all. But the truth is, John, we are just stewards. He trusts us with it."

No Problem Too Big

Recently I entered the Crystal Cathedral with Bob Jani and pointed out to him that the entrance to this cathedral has the lowest ceiling of any chapel or church in the United States. The ceiling in my home is eight feet, six inches high. I cannot touch it with my fingertips. But the ceilings under the balconies in the cathedral are only seven feet high. I can lay my hands flat on the ceiling, it's so low. So it is thrilling to step from under the low balconies into the awesome expanse of the main sanctuary. It's like a reminder that nobody is too small to touch God. And no problem is too big for His power.

Prayer Talk

I remember a time when I was going down a mountain, flat on my back, in an ambulance, with broken bones and bleeding kidneys. I had had a fall in the mountains and I was hurting. I began to pray. I used two-way communication, saying, "Lord, why in the world did I fall, anyway?" And I heard Him say, *Schuller, it's your own miserable fault. You shouldn't have sat on such a rickety ladder.*

"That's right, Lord. That's right. It's my own fault. Lord,

I hope I'm not too badly injured." I heard Him say, *Don't worry. You've got two kidneys and only one is hurting. You'll be okay.* And so it went all the way down the mountain, over an hour in the ambulance. The attendant said to me, "Don't you want a shot?" And I answered, "No, I'm having too good a time talking with God."

Your Most Important Decision

I've been in churches where I have heard ministers preach the toughest sermons I've ever heard. They scold people, they rebuke people, they slap their hands and pound their fists; they give them verbal crucifixions from the pulpit. I've thought, *How can these people take such a verbal whipping? This minister is just tearing the people down. How can they take it? They're going to walk out any minute. They're going to hate that preacher!* And you know what? I was totally wrong. I lingered in the back and heard the people say to the pastor, "Oh, that was a great sermon, Reverend." I couldn't get over it!

Then I began to analyze it. I looked at the faces of the people, and do you know what I saw? I saw people who do not understand what the grace of God means! They have to earn their forgiveness. They want to pay for their own sins. They want to be verbally spanked so they won't feel guilty anymore. They don't understand that Christ died on the cross and paid the whole deal! All we have to do is accept!

Man's biggest problem is that he hates himself. God's toughest job is to make you believe that you can be a beautiful person. Your most important decision is in choosing— choosing to accept God's forgiveness and choosing to take God into your life.

Trust the God Who Loves You

It happened January 6, 1982. He was driving through the Grenalla Pass, going from his home in Bailey, Colorado, to Georgetown, Colorado. His name was Allen Phillips. He could easily make the trip at the 11,665-foot elevation. He was expecting the road to be clear, so he had no chains on his tires. Suddenly an enormous storm struck, and Allen found himself in a blizzard. He was hopelessly stuck. Darkness fell and he knew the road was closed. There was no way he could get out. He didn't have enough gas to keep the car running, and he knew that by morning he would be dead. Then a thought came into his mind—a crazy, impossible thought.

He remained cool. He did not panic. Here was the idea: He would use the headlights of the car to signal an S.O.S.—three shorts, three longs, and three shorts. Even though he was surrounded by trees and mountains, maybe somebody would see.

A Rocky Mountain Airline commuter flight happened to be flying high overhead and one passenger, the local deputy sheriff, who knew the Morse code, just happened to be looking out the window. He thought he saw three shorts, three longs, three shorts. He went to the pilot and said, 'I think I've seen a Morse code in headlights." The captain then made a swing around and indeed, he saw three shorts, three longs, three shorts. The captain radioed the Federal Aviation Administration. The FAA called the Clear Creek sheriff's station. They sent out two snow vehicles and they rescued the stranded man!

Understanding Christianity

Sigmund Freud came to America in 1908. He was very distressed that the Americans mistranslated his words. But after his visit, he went back to Germany and made this profound statement: "Psychoanalysis will survive unless it is accepted without being understood." And I say the same thing about Christianity. Christianity will survive unless it is accepted without being understood.

What do I mean? Christianity is accepted by many people as a good way of life; a nice philosophy; an interesting set of ethics; a basically wholesome moral system; culturally quite refined. It is accepted, but not understood. Do you want to understand it? If you want to understand it, this is what is involved: I say to Jesus Christ, "I'm willing to sacrifice myself; my pride; my glory; my honor; my name. And I want You to live in me and through me. I will die. Jesus, you can live in this brain, thinking my thoughts; in this face, smiling at people; in this heart, loving the lonely; and I will never expect any credit." That's understanding Christianity and that's power!

Always There

I'll never forget when I took my oldest daughter, Sheila, to the airport. She left home to go to college. Then my second child, my son, finally had to leave home. I took him to the airport; he flew to Holland, Michigan, to go to Hope College. Then my third child, Jeanne, left. She took the plane to Chicago. She chose Wheaton College. Recently Carol, our seventeen-year-old, left home. She's got a few medals in her room that she picked up at the National Skiing Championships in Colorado. When she saw the movie *Chariots of Fire* she said, "Dad, I want to try to make the handicapped Olympic team." And she explained, "You know, every time there's an Olympics, there's also a division for the handicapped. And the next international Olympics happen in 1984."

So, all by herself these past months, she was thinking and praying. She thought she had a shot at making the team in 1984, but she said, "In order to do that, Dad, I really have to start training. I have to spend a few hours every day, five days a week, on the slopes with a good coach." She said, "Dad, I've lined up a coach in Winter Park, Colorado. And I've written to Sacramento so I can be released from high school and can continue my courses through correspondence, and not become a dropout." She had solutions to all the problems.

"And so," she said, "I've been calling around and I think maybe I can even find a room I can rent." And, well, you know, we believe in possibility thinking at our home, so we didn't discourage her. We took her to the airport. Three

134

suitcases. Her skis. Her outriggers. We kissed her good-bye. And she left home for Winter Park, Colorado.

I called her before church one morning. She was getting ready to go to church, herself. I asked, "Can I tell the people what you're doing?" She said sure. I said, "Of course if I tell them, then you can't come home in two weeks."

Let's face it, she wasn't gone twenty-four hours and she called up and said, "I miss you, Mom and Dad." I told her, "Well, most of the time you were in your room and the door was closed. You never talked that much." She said, "No, but I knew you were there all the time."

I said, "That's a little the way it is with God, isn't it?"

A Promise

There was a Scottish lassie who was dying. When some-body came to her and asked, "Lassie, where are you going?" she replied, "I'm going to heaven."

"How can you be so sure you're going to heaven?" She said, "Oh, He promised. He said, 'I will not leave you.' That's good enough for me." The person asked, "But what if He forgets His promise?" The lassie said, "He'd lose more than I would. I'd only lose my soul, but he'd lose His honor."

"I will not leave you comfortless"—that's a promise of Jesus!

Break Away From Defensive Holding

I was in Washington recently and I talked to a father who had two daughters in high positions on Capitol Hill. I said to the father, "How did you ever manage to have two daughters in such powerful positions on Capitol Hill?" And his answer was, "I used to take them to the capital when they were little girls so they could see the seat of power. One daughter graduated from high school and I wanted her to go to college. But she said, 'I'm going to get a job—I'm going to become secretary to a great senator!' " The father said, "I didn't want to let her go. I didn't dare let my two daughters leave home and go to the city without having chaperones or protection."

I asked him who gave in and this is what he told me: "I'm a football fan, Dr. Schuller, and about that time I was watching football and I saw my favorite team get a red penalty flag. They were penalized for defensive holding. It was like a message from God saying, *Father, don't be penalized for defensive holding. Don't hold your daughters back! Let them go! Let them fly like birds! Let them be what they were designed to be!*"

Some of you are being penalized for defensive holding. God has a plan for your life. God has a dream for you. His ideas come to you and they are always big. They are always beautiful, but they always seem to be impossible. So, because they threaten your success, you hold back. Because there's a possibility of failure, you don't move ahead.

What would you be trying to do today if you knew you

could not fail? The difference between a person at the top of the ladder and a person at the bottom of the ladder is that the person at the top never penalizes himself for defensive holding.

A Special Evening Walk

I made a return trip to Mainland China a few years ago. My son led a tour of people who were invited to be a part of that mission. One night I tapped on my son's door. We were in Shanghai. It was rather late, but Bob was not in his room. Someone said, "He went out for a walk."

I immediately went out into the street to see if I could spot him. I saw a crowd, almost a mob, gathered on the bridge. I cautiously approached the large group of Chinese who surrounded the six-foot-four-inch-tall American. It was my son. Bob was talking to two of the leaders of this great crowd. I could see that he was excitedly sharing with these two.

Afraid of intruding, I quietly retreated to the hotel. Later that night he told me what happened. He was on the bridge when the group came up to him. There were two bright students who spoke English. They asked him, "Who are you? Where are you from? What are you doing here?"

He said, "Have you ever heard about Jesus Christ?"

"No."

"Well," he said, "I'm a Christian."

They asked, "What's a Christian?"

He told them, and he led them through the spiritual laws. He explained that it is a law that God wants us all to be beautiful persons. It's a law of life that we all have our sins, our internal tensions. We all need salvation. And then he said, "Jesus came to save us."

He asked them if they'd like to accept Jesus as their Friend. To his amazement, they said, "Yes."

So Bob prayed with them. There on the street in Shanghai, Bob and the young Chinese students prayed together. Bob had told them about the Bible, so in response to their request he later sent them Bibles and continued corresponding with them.

That Floyd River

I was born on a little farm in Iowa and I remember fishing in a river near the house. When I look at rivers I usually find myself asking these questions: Where's the source of the river? What is the course of the river? What is the force of the current?

You know that Floyd River of Iowa doesn't realize it, but it flows into the big Sioux. And the big Sioux doesn't know it, but it flows into the Missouri. And the Missouri flows into the Mississippi. And the Mississippi creates a massive fruit-bearing area called the Delta—the fertile farmland of the South. Someday I wish that profitable, fruitful, superproductive Mississippi Delta could stand up and with a warm southern drawl say, "Hats off to you, Floyd River, Iowa!" They may not realize it in the Delta, but they owe something to the Floyd River in Iowa.

The little stream flows into the big stream. You need the same Christ in you that I have in me to be your Source, to set your course, and to be a Force in your life.

"Walk Humbly With Your God"

I think everybody who attended the 1984 Presidential Prayer Breakfast in Washington, D.C. had wet eyes at one point. It was not the remarkable and beautiful talk by our president, Ronald Reagan, and it was not the address given by a marvelous speaker, Barbara Jordan. But it happened when Senator Jacob Javitz read the Old Testament lesson.

Senator Javitz is suffering from ALS, or as it is most commonly known, Lou Gehrig's disease. I happened to have a table up in front. I was able to see the sparkle in his eye.

There were pillows propped behind his back and he had a breathing apparatus with a plastic tube that allowed him to breathe.

Between gasps of breath, he read: "What does the Lord require of you but to be just, to love mercy, and walk humbly with your God."

Then he said, "My favorite chapter in the Bible is Psalm 23":

The Lord is my shepherd, I shall not want. He makes me to lie down in green pastures. He leads me beside the still waters. . . . Even though I walk through the valley of the shadow of death, I will fear no evil, for thou art with me. Thy rod and thy staff, they comfort me. Thou preparest a table before me in the presence of mine enemies. Surely goodness and mercy shall follow me all the days of my life and I shall dwell in the house of the Lord forever.

Senator Javitz knows it. Jesus has a way of coming into our lives and He deals with our contradictions. Somehow He integrates us, consolidates us, takes the opposing movements, and creates the cross out of them. We rise with a life so amazing, so divine, so abundant, so eternal.

What If?

A while back, I was in San Francisco riding on a cable car. Halfway up the hill the cable car lost power. Everybody had to get out of the car and walk the rest of the way up the hill. Many people fear this in their own lives. They don't dare to make a commitment. They're thinking, *What if the power runs out before I get to the top of the hill?*

Not long ago, I was flying with a friend of mine. We were in his private plane, coming back from Cabo San Lucas. The pilot and my friend, who is also a pilot, were up front, and I was in the back with my son. It was a nice, relaxing plane ride. The weather was beautiful. The Sea of Cortez below us was a gorgeous turquoise and green. There was nothing but sea to the right, to the left, ahead, and behind us. I was studying and reading and doing a lot of work. As I lifted my eyes, I saw the pilot suddenly throw some switches. Then I heard him say, "Would you see if the owner's manual is in the glove compartment?"

I got nervous. My friend opened it and said, "Yeah, here it is." The pilot said, "Check this problem out. What do we do if—I think it's on page fourteen." I interrupted, "How far are we from land? What if the motor fails before you are over the landing strip?"

What if the power stops halfway up the hill? What if the motor goes before the landing strip is below you? What if the top rung of the ladder breaks before you've reached the roof? What if the sound system fails before you've finished the sermon?

Strength to see you through to the end. That is what God promises and that's what God provides. Be confident of this one thing: that God, who has begun a good work in you, will complete it. That is how God carries us—with a dream, with a decision, a desire, and finally with the determination never to stop trusting Him, even if the motor may be misfiring.

A Very Positive Statement

I did some traveling one summer, and it was amazing. I was not able to escape the Crystal Cathedral. First, I went through Germany and opened *Sterne* magazine (which is like *Life* magazine in the United States), and there was the Crystal Cathedral. Not long after, I found myself flying Japan Airlines. I pulled out their monthly magazine and saw a picture of the Crystal Cathedral. I found myself, not too many weeks later, in Shanghai, downtown in the heart of modern communism. And I made contact with a very important Chinese official who is best left unnamed and unidentified. We met privately on Sunday in my hotel room, and he shared many things with me that cannot be repeated. But he also said, "Would you like to go to church with me tomorrow?"

He explained, "A church has just been opened—it has been closed, you know, for twenty-seven years. Actually it's just around the corner from the consulate—a very important location." I said, "I'd love to attend." And I went with him.

As we approached the church, my friend said, "You know, they may recognize you here." I said, "Oh, really?"

"Yes," he replied. "Your picture is up on the wall. I'll show you."

So we walked past the consulate where our government had erected a large, glass-covered poster on the wall that encircles the consulate offices. There were pictures and scenes of the United States which the consulate felt would make a great impression upon the millions of modern Chinese who walk down the street. Included was the largest picture of yours truly standing in the Crystal Cathedral. I asked my friend, "What does it say under the photo?" He said, "It says, 'Americans are happy people—they believe in God. Faith is very much alive.' " He continued, " 'In fact, not long ago, one of the most beautiful churches built in America was erected and made out of ten thousand, six hundred, sixty-eight windowpanes.' "

The Crystal Cathedral was used by the federal government of the United States to hopefully make a positive statement of faith to China.

The Lord Is Alive

A dear friend of mine was the president of Hope College in Holland, Michigan, when I was there in my undergraduate days. Many years ago, he and his young son were taking a trip from Michigan when an accident happened. As my friend tells it, suddenly the icy roads caused the car to flip over into a ditch. He lost consciousness. It was very cold and snowing heavily. He wondered if he'd even survive. He awoke and found himself being held in the arms of his little boy, his own heavy body resting against the child's tiny chest. The boy was crying—crying and praying. He said, "Dear Jesus, don't let my daddy die.

He's a good man, and does a lot of good for a lot of people. Dear Jesus, don't let my daddy die." And then my friend saw a Presence. He said, "There, next to my son, as clearly as I saw my son I saw Him, the Lord. And I wanted to go with Him so badly. I wanted to rush to Him and be with Him forever. And there was my little boy begging me to stay."

He said, "Bob, the skeptics can say what they want, the doubters can say what they will, the unbelievers can make their speeches. Me, I am an educator, I am a rationalist, I am a humanist, I am a scientist, and I have to tell you, I know I saw the Lord. And He's alive!"

Never Say Lost

Many years ago, when my friend Doris Day's husband died, I said to her, "I am so sorry that you lost your husband." Boy, did she straighten me out. She said, "Bob, don't ever use that word *lost!* That is a negative word. When you hear the word *lost* the subconscious thinks of all kinds of nonrecallable experiences. I lost a coin, I lost a job, I lost this, I lost that. Never use that word *lost.* I have not lost my husband. I have agreed to let God accept him in faith."

My Best Friend

I remember when I made a speech a few years ago in Saint Louis, Missouri. I came to town and was in my hotel at five o'clock in the afternoon. I was scheduled to go on the stage at half-past six to deliver a speech at a big, important convention. I unpacked my suit, which I hadn't worn in four months. I had lost thirty-eight pounds in those four months. My waist had dropped four inches. The trousers required a belt, and I had neglected to pack one. Possibly I could have made it through the lecture if I'd been the kind of speaker who never raised his arms.

I looked for a big safety pin which, of course, I couldn't find. I looked for a wire clothes hanger, thinking I could open it up and use it as a belt. That idea did not work. I called the front desk and asked, "Is there a tailor in town?" They said, "The tailor in the mall might still be open." I quickly trotted there and went in with my pair of trousers. He looked at me with that "We are about to close up" look. I said, "Can you take my trousers in for me?" He said, "Sure, but it will take a couple of hours."

I said to him, "They told me at the hotel that you are the greatest tailor in town. Is that true?"

"Well, I have been at it a long time."

"I have a friend in Orange, California, who could do this job for me in twenty minutes. You say that it'll take you two hours?"

He said, "Your tailor can do it in twenty minutes? We can do it in eighteen!"

He fixed the pants for me while I waited. They fit great. I said to him, "I knew you could do it! I've got faith."

He said, "You sound like a religious guy. In fact, haven't I seen you someplace?"

I said, "Could be."

"Are you a minister?"

"Yes."

"What's your religion like, anyway?"

I said, "Well, first of all, it's not really a religion in the sense that most religions are—made up of rules and regulations—don't do this and don't do that. It's not restriction, don't go here, don't go there. And it's not just a ritual where we recite the same memorized prayers. If it's not regulations, restrictions, or rituals, then what is it? It's a relationship that I have with Somebody who's become my Best Friend. His name is Jesus Christ. I believe in Him."

It's the Regularity That Counts

Not long ago I was running and my path crossed with a man whose name many of you know. His name is George Romney. He was once the governor of Michigan. We ran together for about a mile.

I said, "When did you get into physical fitness so seriously?"

"I was in a physical-fitness program up in Wisconsin and there was a banner in the athletic center. The banner said, 'It's not the amount, it's the regularity that counts.' "

Then he added, "You know, Bob, that's true in prayer life. It's true in your walk with the Lord. It's not how many minutes you spend praying every day. It's not how many chapters of the Bible you have read. Yes, we have to pray every day. Yes, we have to read the Scriptures every day.

But it's not how many hours we spend on our knees. It's not the amount, it's the regularity that counts. If you're regular and faithful in your prayer and in your walk with Him, you'll know what God's will for your life is. You'll know what He wants you to do."

Play with the dream. Pray about the dream constantly, then pay the price. God isn't going to call you out of the security corner only to see you fall flat on your face. Rather, He calls you out of the corner to take a chance, but then He expects you to pay the price.

If you're in business, you pay the price through excellence of product, excellent service, and excellent treatment of people. It's easy to succeed if you treat people nicely.

God Is Sometimes Silent

An amusing incident happened to me recently. I lectured on Tuesday at the University of Berkeley and on Wednesday I was scheduled to speak to the Lutherans at the five-hundredth anniversary of Martin Luther's birthday in Arizona. On Thursday, I was to be at Northwestern University of Iowa, and on Friday I had to be at Johns Hopkins in Baltimore. As you can see, it was really a tightly scheduled week. Everything was carefully timed and planned. If I missed a connection, I would really be in trouble.

Everything went smoothly until I got to Phoenix to catch my eastbound plane. I was first at the check-in desk, to make sure I would not be late. Soon there was a line of about thirty or forty people behind me with all their suitcases, waiting to check in. The plane was scheduled to leave in thirty minutes. Eventually a lady came to start the check-in. She looked harried. Trying to be understanding, I said, "You look like you have troubles."

She didn't even look up to see my face. She just mumbled, "Boy, have I got troubles!" She said, "I suppose you're here to check on this flight to Denver."

I said, "Yes."

She said, "Well, I just got word that that flight's going to be canceled, and I suppose you are now going to want me to help you, which I'm obligated to do, but I don't know what I'm going to do!" And then she looked up and said, "Oh, Dr. Schuller!" And she took hold of my hands and said, "Say a little prayer for me. I'm in trouble. I don't know what I'm going to do. Let me talk to the computer a minute."

She began to type on the keyboard. She stopped and looked at the computer. Her face registered dismay and frustration. Frantic, she picked up the phone. "Ben! Help! The computer's dead! Nothing! It's just looking at me. You say we have a line problem? I don't care if it's a line problem. Make it come alive, please!" She hung up.

The point is this: Before you complain because God is silent, remember, every once in a while, the computers are silent, too. However, you don't stop believing in a computer because there's a line condition. And we don't stop believing in God because there's a line problem.

"Help! Is Anybody Up There?"

One day I was in a distant city when I met a man who told me how he had been converted. His life had been completely and totally changed. "I can't tell you the kind of dirty, unclean, demeaning life I was living," he said. "I just want to tell you that since I've become a Christian, my whole moral life has changed. I am a different person. In fact," he said, "I was converted listening to one of your jokes."

"What was the joke?" I asked. And he told me the story of a fellow who had dropped off a cliff and was plummeting toward the rocks below when he managed to grasp the twig of a tree that was growing through a crack in the granite cliff. Hanging there, hundreds of feet above the sharp granite rocks and swirling white water below, he looked up into the clouds that hid the edge of the cliff from his sight and cried, "Help! Is anybody up there?" And out of the clouds came the words, *I am here.* "Who are you?" he questioned. *I am your God,* the voice replied. "Can you help me?" the man asked in a voice tinged with desperation. *Have faith,* the heavenly voice commanded. *Let go.* The man looked down at the jagged rocks, then looked up toward the clouds and shouted, "Is anybody else up there?"

Fannie May's Advice

I will never forget the time I was in the airport in Chicago, Illinois, and I stopped in the Fannie May Candy Store. My wife likes candy; I don't eat it. I actually think it's bad for your health. It's against my religion, but not hers!

I went into the store and there was another customer there—an old lady with a bag, a bunch of gifts, and a little suitcase. She looked very disorganized and somewhat ruffled. She was looking at the counter and since the clerk was waiting for her to decide what she wanted, I said to the clerk, "Do you have chocolate-covered nuts in one-pound boxes?" Before the clerk could respond, the little lady answered, "Oh, sure, they have chocolate-covered nuts in one-pound boxes; they also have them in two- and three-pound boxes, and they are very good." The clerk said, "Yes, that's right. We do have chocolate-covered nuts in one-pound boxes."

Turning my back to the older lady, I asked the clerk, "Do you by any chance have turtles? You know, the caramel and walnuts with chocolate over them? My wife loves those caramel turtles." Again, before the clerk could answer, the busybody said, "Oh, sure, they have turtles in one-, two-, and three-pound boxes." The clerk appeared somewhat annoyed, and then the old lady said, "I'd advise you to buy a one-pound box of the Colonial assortment. It has chocolate-covered nuts, the turtles, and the creams, too." I answered, "My wife doesn't like creams." She said, "Oh, I think she'd like these creams. These are delicious." I tried to ignore her, but to no avail. She really persisted. It was a very awkward situation until suddenly the woman said, "I have to go or I'll miss my plane." She quickly gathered her bundles and suitcase and walked out. I breathed a sigh of relief and so did the clerk. Then she turned around and shouted to the back room, "Okay, girls, you can come out now. Fannie May is gone!"

I said, "Fannie May! That was Fannie May?" She answered, "Yes. Her name is not really Fannie May. Her husband died and left her with a candy store. She decided that instead of feeling sorry for herself, she would invent some new chocolates. So she made up all of these recipes herself, opened more stores, and today she has one hundred seventeen stores. All she does is fly around the country and check on her stores. She calls them her one hundred seventeen children."

I was looking at the clerk as an authority, when the real authority was right there! How sad. You know, some of you, in the same way, look to Dr. Schuller or some other minister to interpret the Bible. Let Jesus Christ be the Authority. Don't look to me—look to Him. If you really want to feel good about yourself, Christ says you must value life most highly in yourself and in others. You look upon every seed as a tremendous potential. Then you'll love life. You'll love the Lord, your God, your neighbor, and yourself. With that much love, what a beautiful community of human beings we can become.

"Take Me to Christ's Church"

I once said to Dr. Viktor Frankl that even meaning is meaningless unless it feeds my self-esteem because the deepest need (deeper than sensuality, deeper than status or power, deeper than significance) is self-esteem. I have to feel as if I am worth something and so do you. Don't let people put you down and say you're on an ego trip. Look, if a person has no ego needs, that person is sick. The ego needs stem from our deep need to feel worthy, and Jesus Christ does this. That's why He's still the most popular Person in the world today.

I was told that somebody came out to California recently and picked a cab. The man said to the cabdriver, "Take me to Christ's church," so the cabdriver took him all the way to Orange County and dropped him off at the Crystal Cathedral. The man said, "I said Christ's church!" (There is a Church of Christ in Garden Grove). You know what the cabdriver said? "If He's in town, He'll be there!"

Don't Carry the Truth Too Far

If you have the faith of a grain of a mustard seed you can say to this mountain, "Move," and nothing will be impossible to you. The philospher George Santayana said, "Anytime somebody has a truth, somebody else will come along and carry it too far." I have been in this work for about thirty years, and I get letters, I meet people, and I know there are people who carry possibility thinking too far.

Not long ago I read a tragic story of people of another faith who believed that if they had enough faith, nothing was impossible. They interpreted that to mean that when a loved one died, if they prayed and had faith, the dead person would come to life. So when their child died, they did just that. Days passed while they prayed. Finally the body was decomposed and the officials moved in. How tragic.

A man once told me that when someone suffered the amputation of a limb, we need to pray, and believe that the limb will grow back. I totally disagree. That kind of faith does not glorify God! It insults the intelligence of His brightest creatures—you and me. God is not glorified through human insults.

EXTRAORDINARY COURAGE

Break Your Record

I recently took time for rest and renewal. After a grueling schedule I went to Hawaii with my wife. When we go there, we always run. For many years, I have run from the Kahala Hilton Hotel to Diamond Head and back, which is four and one-quarter miles. If I run from the hotel to the lighthouse on Diamond Head and back, I've run precisely five miles.

That's as far as I ever run in Hawaii. That's because if I wanted to run farther I would have energy and power that I never tapped before and never knew was there. This time, my breathing didn't go half-cycle—it went full-cycle with every breath. It was magnificent to feel the body working like a marvelous, finely tuned machine.

I felt like a million bucks. I was running and I was only about a half mile from the hotel. Now I had gone six and a half miles and I had set a new record, and broken through what had been a mental barrier in my life for twelve years. I found a tennis ball in the gutter, picked it up, and started dribbling.

At that point, I met a crusty, old, retired army general who is well known in Hawaii. He was riding his high-speed racing bike. He saw me and recognized me. Knowing that I'd had some problems, he said, "Don't let them get you down, Reverend."

What a lift he gave me. Don't let anybody get you down. Don't let anything get you down. Don't let any problems, don't let any obstacle, don't let any difficulty get you down. Break into new dimensions. Set the record. Let me give you a line right now: "If it's going to be, then it's up to me."

Saved by the Mystery Doctor

A dear friend of mine, Algetha Brown, is a beautiful singer. In my opinion, she's one of the great black women singers in America. Algetha is married to an air force career man. Right after the Second World War, they were assigned to Germany.

The Nuremberg trials were happening. As Algetha said, "At that time there were many scared German citizens, because the word was out that if you were a Nazi or if you were a close friend of the Gestapo or if you were a good friend of a Nazi, the odds were that you might be called in for questioning. You might be arrested. You could be put on trial, sent to jail, and even to death if you were involved in the Holocaust."

She said, "Dr. Schuller, my husband and I met so many good, beautiful, wonderful German people who weren't Nazis, but they knew the wrong people so they were in hiding."

At the time, Colonel Brown, his wife, Algetha, and their two sons were living on the fourth floor of an apartment building. One day, her oldest son came down with the mumps. Algetha kept him in his room. Since it was a warm day, his window was open. Soon the little boy got restless, walked over to the window, sat on the sill, and watched the changing scenes on the street below.

Suddenly a gust of wind came and slammed the shutter, throwing the boy off balance. He fell four floors, ripping through a balcony iron railing two floors below, and landing on a cobblestone street. In a matter of minutes, the ambulance picked up the unconscious boy and brought him to the nearest civilian hospital.

Because he was a military officer's son the military doctors came and examined the boy, finding multiple compound fractures on the right arm. Even though he was not conscious, they could find no internal injury. Everything seemed to be okay, but they said that the arm would have to be amputated. There was no way it could be saved.

When the doctors left the room Algetha cried at her little boy's side and looked at the arm that would be coming off in twenty-four hours. The nurse, a German woman, walked up to Algetha, put her arm around her, looked at the beautiful little boy, unconscious on the bed, and said, "I probably shouldn't say this, but I know a German doctor who might be able to save that arm. I don't know if he'll come. He's in hiding. He had the wrong friends during the war. I do know where he's hiding."

Algetha said, "Would you ask him?"

Late that night Algetha was almost asleep at the bedside of her little boy, praying for his surgery in the morning, when a stranger in shabby clothes entered the room, looking furtively around. Seeing no one other than Algetha, he walked up to the bedside. Algetha looked up and asked, "Who are you?"

Whispering, he said, "I am the doctor the nurse talked to you about."

"Oh, thank you for coming!"

The doctor said, "I'm just going to check him. I must leave quickly before people find out I'm here." He checked the arm and said, "Mrs. Brown, that arm could be saved. I could save it."

The distraught young mother said, "Oh, would you, please?"

To her dismay, he said, "I can't. I'm awfully sorry."

She said, "Is it because I'm black?" He didn't even answer her. He merely turned and left the room.

The next morning, as the boy was being prepared for surgery, the nurse came in and said, "Mrs. Brown, I just got a call from the doctor. He said that he can't let them take the boy's arm. He said he would come out of hiding to do it, but we must keep it a secret."

An hour later he was scrubbing up. Two hours later, with the military surgeons standing back, the German doctor went to work. It was the first of seven operations that took out every little piece of stray splintered bone. The arm was saved.

But the news got out about the miracle surgery. Headlines read, "Black American Boy's Amputation Saved by Mystery Doctor."

Investigators read it. They said, "There's only one doctor who could have pulled that off. It's the one we've been looking for." They found him, of course. They arrested him and brought him to trial. He received a sentence of five years in prison.

As he was being led away, handcuffed, Algetha said, "Why did you do it?"

He answered simply, "You always have to do the right thing, no matter what the risk is, don't you?"

That's how to live life and be proud of yourself. Then when you die, you can meet your God, with pride behind you, love around you, and hope ahead of you. Say yes to God. Fantastic things will happen to you. "Blessed are they that hunger and thirst after righteousness, for they shall be satisfied" (see Matthew 5:6).

Miss Terry

I dropped into Milwaukee to give a speech recently. When my friends picked me up at the airport, they said, "Dr. Schuller, you've got to stop and see Miss Terry in the hospital." My schedule was very full, but I consented, so we quickly made a hospital call.

I am so glad I decided to stop and see Miss Terry. I will never forget her. She is a beautiful, young black mother of two children. But her heart is not strong enough to keep her alive. Her only hope of survival is a heart transplant. I prayed with her that God would give her as many years as He could to spend with her children. She hugged me and said, "Dr. Schuller, the program every Sunday morning keeps my hopes up. Thank you for what you're doing."

Miss Terry is only one of a few million people who are counting on me and on you. Jesus said, "Unto whom much is given, much will be required" (see Luke 12:48). There are a lot of people who need to be treated friendly, fairly, frankly, firmly, and faithfully. It has to start with me. And it has to start with you.

The Five Principles of Success

Any success I've achieved in my life I owe to five principles. Before I give them to you, I have to tell you that I learned them from someone wiser than me.

His name was Dr. Henry Poppen. I was only a young boy growing up in northwest Iowa when he came with his dashing tales of derring-do in Mainland China. This brave missionary captured my respect and admiration as he told about the adventures he had with bandits, and his near escape from death on mountain trails as he shared the Good News of Christ with the people of China.

Then came the great conflict between Japan and China, when half a million Chinese refugees escaped to an island without shelter or food. The English government appointed Dr. Henry Poppen to be the governor of those five hundred thousand refugees. I asked him later, "Dr. Poppen, how did you dare to face up to the Japanese general who came to the shore demanding surrender? Instead of being frightened and intimidated by him, you courageously declared, 'I will not surrender.' In fact, you told him to bring you and your people boatloads of soybeans. How did you dare to talk to him that way?"

He said, "Bob, I merely spoke to that Japanese general the way I talk to anybody. I have five words that I live by, and communicate by. They are: First . . . be friendly; second . . . be frank; third . . . be fair; fourth . . . be firm; and fifth . . . be faithful."

Take the Offensive

Recently, when I was visiting Guatemala, I was escorted by a brilliant young man in his early thirties who holds a dual passport to Guatemala and the United States. He shared with me his concern for the country. He said, "Dr. Schuller, Christianity is losing the battle in Guatemala because they're fighting defensively. All of the missionaries have fled. They are afraid of being kidnapped and held for ransom by the Communists, or of being shot down by terrorists. There is no way we can win the fight without changing our tactics from defensive to offensive."

He continued, "Did you know that I served in Vietnam?"

I answered, "No. I was not aware of that."

Then he shared with me this fascinating story. He was an officer in Vietnam, assigned to keeping one area clear of the enemy. Every day he and his men would have to go into the jungle. Every day he saw a casualty or two, even though he approached all battles cautiously.

One day his commanding officer, a colonel, visited. He

said, "Lieutenant, how are you doing? Are you keeping the area clear of the enemy?"

My young friend replied, "I think I'm doing quite well, sir."

The colonel took a look at the lieutenant's casualty count. He shook his head and said, "There are some losses here." Then he looked at the lieutenant and said, "Do you know what you're doing wrong?"

"No, sir."

He said, "You're trying to hold and clear the territory, but you're trying to avoid all contact with the enemy."

"That's correct, sir. I don't want to lose my men. Every life is very valuable, sir."

The colonel said, "Don't tell me that. I know that! Look, you're trying to *hold* the territory, you're not trying to *conquer* the territory. You're fighting defensively. I'm giving you a command right now to go out there and contact the enemy at any time and any point you can."

My young friend looked at his commander and said, "Sir, with all due respect, may God help my men. I don't know how many lives I'd lose."

But the colonel only looked firmly at the young man and said, "That's a command!" With that he got into his helicopter. The blades whirled slowly, then faster and faster. As he took off, the lieutenant looked at his staff sergeant, who had heard the whole conversation. He said, "Sergeant, did you hear that? That colonel must be a crazy man. 'Go out there and contact the enemy!' How many bodies will I have to count tomorrow night?"

The sergeant said, "Sir, may I say something? With all due respect, I think the colonel is right. Look at how many casualties we've had this past month."

The lieutenant said, "Well, if you think he's right, and if the colonel is commanding me, I guess I have no choice but to change my strategy."

The next morning they went on the offensive. There were several casualties. The second day they plunged deeper and took more casualties than they usually had in an average week. But on the fourth day there were no casualties. The fifth day they went deeper into the jungle.

Again there were no casualties. The sixth day they penetrated as far as they could, and still there were no casualties. On the seventh and eighth days they couldn't even find the enemy. The lieutenant said to the sergeant, "What happened to the enemy?"

The sergeant replied, "Sir, I think the enemy has gone off to fight somebody who's fighting on the defensive."

Pebbles Make Up the Beaches of the World

Penny Cotton, a young woman who attended the National Women's Conference at the Crystal Cathedral recently, suffered a stroke when she was twenty-seven years old. It almost killed her, and left her paralyzed. Because of the paralysis she did not want to live, so she planned to commit suicide. Then she tuned in the "Hour of Power" and through the happy faces and joyful music she received hope. That was enough to change her from suicidal thoughts. She became a possibility thinker. Why? Because she found comfort. She committed her life to Jesus Christ and dared to believe she could earn her own way in life and not be dependent on others. That's exactly what she did. She became a life insurance salesperson. In gratitude to God, she dared to believe she could save enough dollars to buy a star in the Crystal Cathedral. She shared with me last week and said, "You know, Dr. Schuller, I'm just a little pebble." I said to her, "Penny, if there were no pebbles, there would be no beaches. The pebbles make up the beaches of the world!"

Job's Representative

A while ago I received a letter from a gentleman. He identified himself as Dallas J. Anderson and enclosed his resume, which was very impressive. It included undergraduate work in art at Saint Olaf College in Minnesota, and nine years of graduate work in sculpture at the Royal Danish Academy of Fine Arts. He enclosed a portfolio with photographs of a plaster model of a sculpture he called *Job*. He was planning to reproduce it in bronze. It looked magnificent—like a work of Michelangelo. He said he would like to donate the bronze statue to the gardens of the Crystal Cathedral.

I was thrilled, to say the least, but I wrote him and said, "Thank you, Dallas, but for me the work should be done in marble, not in bronze. It should be carved so that the form will glisten and ripple. I feel that marble sculpting has a humanity that bronze does not. Furthermore, the whole subject is faith versus healing, poverty versus the possibility of prosperity. Such loss and torment would be stated much more strongly if it were in white against a dark base." I asked him, "Can you possibly reproduce this job in marble without losing its emotion?"

He answered, "It's odd that you should request this because last year I was in Vermont, and I purchased this exquisite chunk of white Vermont marble, seven feet high. My answer is, 'Yes! I would love to do it!'"

So for the next year and a half, Dallas Anderson quietly carved away. Finally on Thanksgiving morning 1983, the statue was unveiled. At its base are four verses from the Book of Job. On one side, carved in dark granite, is the text, "The Lord gave, the Lord has taken away. Blessed be the name of the Lord" (*see* Job 1:21). On the other side,

163

"Though he slay me yet will I trust him" (*see* Job 13:15). On another, "I know my Redeemer lives" (*see* Job 19:25). And on the fourth side, "When he has tried me I shall come forth as gold" (*see* Job 23:10).

Who needs to be tried? We all do. The truth is that every day is a trial. If you're in business, you know what I'm talking about. You are tried in the marketplace every day and the customer either likes your product or he doesn't. You come forth either as gold or as tin, depending upon the quality of product and service you offer.

The Courage to Try

I ran into a young man in an airport in Texas. He happened to be carrying a copy of my book *Tough Times Never Last, But Tough People Do*. He recognized me. He came up to me and said, "Can I have your autograph?"

I was glad to give it.

He said, "Dr. Schuller, this book has really been helping me, because I'm in absolute bankruptcy. I started my own business, but I've lost everything I ever had."

He had a tear in his eye, but continued. "You know, my business was going pretty well. I expanded, with a new plant and more equipment. I was making quite a bit of money. Suddenly the other people who owed me money didn't pay. The little businesses went down the tubes. Then, a couple of big businesses went down the tubes. I looked at my Accounts Receivable and suddenly everything that I had expected to take in had evaporated. My Accounts Receivable were worth nothing. When that happened, I went under, too! That's where I am today. But I saw this book and it's helping."

I said, "Well, first of all, sir, let me correct you. You haven't lost everything you had."

He said, "Oh, but I have."

I said, "No, I don't think so. You haven't lost everything you had. You had something before you had a business. You had a dream. And you had the nerve to try. You haven't lost that."

He said, "I think I have."

I said, "Oh, no! Nobody ever loses courage! Courage isn't something you lose, because courage is always an option."

Courage is a choice. And it's always there for you to choose. You can choose to start over. And remember—every competitor is a winner! Nobody who competes can ever be a total loser, because the total loser is the guy who didn't dare to try. Every competitor is a winner, because he has courage.

Never, never, never, believe that God wants you to be a failure. There may be a round when you get knocked down. There may be a season that is not good. You may go through a really tough period. But just because you've lost the battle doesn't mean you will lose the war.

EXTRAORDINARY LOVE

Every Blessing Is a Burden

I remember when Gretchen, my youngest daughter, asked me to buy her a puppy for Christmas. "Honey," I said, "we've already got two dogs." We have a little acreage, so there is room for the dogs to run. Besides, they are trained for security purposes. After several days of begging, I finally consented. In a weak moment, I said yes. Well, when Carol, my older daughter, found out I was going to buy Gretchen a puppy, she started in on me. "Daddy, I asked you for a puppy three years ago and you said no. I asked you the next year and you still said no. And now you are letting Gretchen have one? That's not fair!" So in another weak moment I said, "Okay, Carol, you can have one, too."

Every blessing is a burden! I now have two puppies! I have lost my kitchen because it's the only room in the house that doesn't have carpeting. (And it's the only room suitable for training puppies.) But the puppies are beautiful and the children love them. (So do I, unfortunately.) I can't help but love the little darlings. A couple of little blessings—but they are a burden!

"God Loves You and So Do I"

Every Sunday I ask members of my congregation to turn around and shake hands with somebody near them and say, "God loves you and so do I!" And just about every week I see a few people with gloomy expressions who reluctantly turn to the persons next to them, shake hands, and say, "God loves you and so do I." And do you know what? When they turn back around and face me, a light comes on! They are smiling and their faces are actually bright!

The most tragic blind spot in any personal philosophy of life is the concept that "if I'm greedy I'll get ahead." Nothing could be further from the truth. "Whatever a man sows, that shall he also reap" (*see* Galatians 6:7).

Still Singing

I recently conducted a funeral service for the man who has been at my side longer than any other person, except for my wife. I graduated from seminary in June of 1950. My first assignment was at a little church of thirty-three members in Chicago, Illinois. The church was divided. It was split because of some contradictions. The people didn't know how to resolve them. They never learned that the lion could lie down with the lamb.

I went to that little church. The ruling elder, the vice-president of the church, was Bain Fisher. He met me at the depot. That was the beginning of a dear friendship. Together we worked to save that church. And I must say, we were successful.

Five years later, the Reformed Church in America, the oldest denomination in the United States of America, invited me to come to California and start a new church. Before I accepted, I wanted to go out there and look over the place. But the denomination didn't have the money to send me. When Bain Fisher, who worked for the Santa Fe Railroad, found out about it, he said, "I don't want to lose you, but you ought to check it out." And he gave me a round-trip train ticket.

Fifteen years ago, Bain joined me in California. What a faithful, loyal servant he has been to our church.

He was my friend for thirty-three years. Then he got lung cancer some months ago. Then they found cancer in the brain. Soon after, we got the call that he passed away quietly. I asked his wife, Charlotte, "Was he conscious at the end?"

She said, "Not quite to the end. He fell asleep about four hours before he passed away, but up until then he was still singing."

I said, "Singing? What was he singing?"

She said, "Oh, his favorite songs. He sang, 'Jesus loves me! this I know,' and "O how I love Jesus, O how I love Jesus, O how I love Jesus because He first loved me!' "

The Magnificent Madonna

I have a friend in Chicago named Don Paset. He owns the largest art and antique store, the Donrose Galleries, on the North Shore. When I visited the art gallery recently, I wandered through its garden. There was a life-size, very stylized, modern bronze statue of the Madonna. There is no face. You supply the features with your imagination. Yet there is no doubt that it's the Madonna.

I was really struck by how beautiful she was. I asked Don how much he wanted for her. He said, "She's not for sale. It's a very, very, important piece by an important contemporary sculptor." I continued to study her beauty. Where the womb would be, there is a hollow in the bronze. In the hollow is a large number six. It, of course, represents the unborn infant. The top of the six represents the head, and the rest of the body of the six represents the body of the unborn child.

As I looked at the statue a young woman near me asked, "Dr. Schuller, why is the baby shaped like a six?"

I said, "I don't know. I didn't talk to the sculptor, but I have my own interpretation that I read into it: On the sixth day, God created Adam and Eve. All of His hopes and dreams were pinned on Adam and Eve. They blew it. So He sent Jesus. When Jesus was born it was as if God went back to the sixth day to try again. He's pinning His last hopes for the human race on Jesus—'The new Adam,' as the Scriptures tell us. 'The second Adam.' God's trying once more."

God Patches Up the Holes

Recently I was in Sioux Falls, South Dakota, where a young couple came up to greet me following a speaking engagement. They held a little baby. They told me how the "Hour of Power" helped them through a terribly difficult time. The young man said, "Three years ago my wife was killed in a tragic car accident." Then the young woman said, "And just thirty days later, my husband was driving at night and was killed in an accident." In unison they said, "God introduced us to each other." As they looked lovingly at each other they said, "Now we're married and it's beautiful! Thank you for 'Hour of Power.' It gives us hope." And then the husband made this classic statement: "God patches up the holes!"

Different Music

I remember the story of the two old Dutchmen, sitting on a park bench. The night had come and the moon started to shine. Not far from the bench where they sat, a river flowed, and from the river came a chorus of crickets. Pete, the first old gentleman, listened to the crickets and said, "Crickets sure do sing." John, sitting next to him, agreed, saying, "Yep, they sure know how to sing." Just then he heard the voices of the choir coming from a nearby church and remarked, "Beautiful music, isn't it?" Pete said, "Yeah, and to think they do it just by rubbing their legs together."

Each heard different music—one was listening to the crickets and one was listening to the choir. What you hear depends on where you're coming from and where you're going! When you come to our church, I want you to hear one thing: the note of real love—the love of Jesus Christ.

The Unknown Singer

Here's a story that I love. It's a true story. It happened in the Paris opera house. A famous singer was planning to sing that night. The house was packed. The curtain was raised. But the singer did not enter the stage. Instead, the house manager stepped to the microphone and made the following announcement: "I am afraid that due to illness the man you've come to hear will not be performing tonight. Someone will be standing in for him." The manager mentioned the stand-in's name, but no one heard it over the groan of disappointment. It was a difficult situation. The unknown singer sang with everything he had. When he finished there was nothing but a stony silence. Suddenly, from one of the high balconies, a little boy stood up and cried, "Daddy, I think you are wonderful!" Then the crowd broke into thunderous applause.

Where do I find my inner security? How do I find my self-esteem? Not through my position. Actually that is a very threatening and vulnerable spot to be in. I don't find self-esteem through performance, because I'm never satisfied with it. Instead, I find it through a Person, a special Person named Jesus Christ. Like that little boy, Jesus says to me, *Schuller, I think you're wonderful.*

Reason to Live

I was asked to visit a young man, twenty-one years of age, who was suicidal. He was living in an institution in Southern California where young men and young women are kept when they are severely mentally handicapped, when there's no hope of recovery.

I went to see him. He said, "Dr. Schuller, I cannot live. I cannot read. I cannot write. My life is totally useless. If I could believe in God, I could live. But I can't believe in God."

I said, "Why not?"

He replied, "Why would God make a useless person like me? I am of no value to anyone."

I was praying for the right answer for this young man, and just then, a nurse walked into our room. I recognized her because she is a member of our church. I remembered talking to her only a few months before when her husband died. She didn't have any income so she was forced to go out and find a job. She had been totally dependent upon her now-deceased husband. Then, suddenly, she had to go back to work at the age of forty-eight. She tried to use her nursing experience, but the hospitals didn't want her. Finally, she took the only nursing job she could find. It was a job at this institution where nobody wanted to work.

Now, here she was. She came bouncing into the room. "Hello, Dr. Schuller! How are you?"

"I'm fine. How are you?"

"Wonderful! I really enjoy this work."

I said, "You do?"

"Oh, yes. I meet the nicest people." Then she came up to the twenty-one-year-old boy whom I was visiting. She tweaked him on the cheek and said, "Johnny, how are you today?"

When he looked up at her, she put her arm around him and said, "Did you know that I really do love you, Johnny?" She looked at me and said, "I don't think he believes that I really do love him. But I do. He's such a sweet guy."

After she left the room, I turned to Johnny and said, "Johnny, your life is not totally useless. You help create a job opportunity for this widow and you help her to forget her own problems. She loves you. Can't you see it?"

He said, "Yeah, I guess so. Do you really think she loves me, Dr. Schuller?"

I said, "Of course, she does!"

Still unconvinced, he said, "Do you really think she loves me, Dr. Schuller?"

I said, "Johnny, I know she does!" I must have said it that time in such a way that he started to cry. I hugged him and he hugged me.

Here was Johnny with an enormous need. And here was a widow with a tremendous need. Two needs collide and a spark ignites. Now that's a principle of life.

Turn Your Problems Into Partners

One of the most inspiring women in our congregation was Sara Rasmussen. I told her story in my book *Move Ahead With Possibility Thinking.* Sara and Norm were about to have their fifth child. They already had four sons, and so they prayed for a girl. At the baby shower the word was, "Think Pink." All the gifts were wrapped in pink paper; all the ribbons were pink. The baby was born and it was a girl. They named her Leah. However, a few months later they found out Leah had Down's syndrome. Nevertheless, they loved her!

They decided not to try to conquer their problem, but to redeem it. They loved little Leah and as she became a junior high school student, she needed peer companionship. So they went to various California adoption agencies and brought mongoloid children nobody else wanted into their home. Soon they had two, three, four, five mongoloid children join their family.

Finally, they moved up to a big old house with lots of empty land where, the last I heard, Sara and her husband and Leah had about twenty-six of these children! They turned their problem into a partner. They're more than conquerors through Christ who loves us.

Beautiful Sammy Brook

Many know the story of Peggy Brook. She already had two little boys when Sammy was born. He was such a beautiful baby. But after a few months, he seemed to have problems with his eyes. She said, "I was so happy when finally I got an apointment with an ophthalmologist." He held up darling little Sammy and looked into one eye. He said the pupil response seemed to be good. Then he looked in the other eye. He said that the voluntary muscle response seemed to be good. But when he looked the third time, his response was silence. Finally he pulled out a chart and said, "The optic nerve is very dull."

Then, without looking at Peggy, he said, "You know, the retina is made up of many little, tiny nerves. They branch into the larger nerves until they converge at the center in the optic nerve. The optic nerve sends all signals to the brain, where they are deciphered. In Sammy's case," he said as he drew some lines to illustrate how we see, "I can't find the little nerves. And the optic nerve is almost nonexistent."

Peggy said, "Will he be able to read?" The doctor answered, "Well, he might be able to see forms. He might be able to tell the difference between light and shadow. At best that will be all he'll be able to see."

Peggy walked out of there holding her little Sammy, her beautiful little baby. And then suddenly, the word came to her: *blind*. Her Sammy was blind! All her hopes turned to ashes. Peggy and her husband wept that night and the next night, and they prayed and held hands and claimed the Bible promises for healing. They asked Jesus, but they got no hope. He never assured them that there would be a healing.

Peggy went through all the emotions: guilt, fear, and anger toward God. But then she remembered what a minister said: "Be positive, thank God anyway." Peggy said, "I began to praise God for Sammy, and Jesus touched me. He didn't touch Sammy. He touched me. In a vision, like a dream, I saw God at the moment of Sammy's conception. I saw Him in heaven holding a beautiful, blond, blue-eyed baby boy. He was looking around the world for a home for this very special baby. He saw a rich man's house, but passed it by. He saw a poor man's house, but He said, *Not there*. Then He saw a home where an unmarried woman did not want a child. He passed her by. And then He saw our little home with the Bible and the cross on the wall. He said, *This is the kind of home that deserves a special gift like Sammy*. And He gave Sammy to me."

Peggy said, "At that moment, all of my negative emotions disappeared. I had nothing but praise to give to God for my beautiful little Sammy—blind, but bright and beautiful!"

The Language of Silence

As you may know, I travel a lot. I was on a plane recently. I overheard the stewardess say, "I've been out of this for a year. I'm just back on the job today."

When she pushed her cart past my seat, I said, "I'm curious. I heard you say that you've been gone for a year. I hope it's been a happy holiday."

Her eyes immediately filled with tears and she said, "No, not really. I lost a little boy."

"Oh, my, I'm sorry." I reached out to her and we gave each other a hug. I asked, "What helped you?"

She said, "So many people meant well, but what they said didn't help me. They said, 'God wanted your little baby, so He took it.' That didn't help—it made me angry at God. Others said, 'Your little baby is now a bud in the bouquet of heaven.' That didn't help me, either. These things help some people, I'm sure. But they didn't help me."

I asked again, "What helped you?"

She said, "A couple came, I really didn't know them. They were Christians. They had lost a little boy, and I knew about their loss. It was tragic, like mine. But when they came, they didn't say anything. They just reached out and hugged me and we cried. That did it."

The silence healed. The stillness helped. For silence has a language all its own.

A Sixty/Forty Proposition

When I was in college, one of the professors said to us, his students, "The secret of a successful marriage is this: Marriage is not a 50/50 proposition. A 50/50 proposition is one where nobody is giving anything.

"Rather, the secret of a happy marriage is 60/40. The husband gives in sixty percent of the time and expects his wife to give in forty percent of the time. The wife gives in sixty percent of the time and expects her husband to give in forty percent of the time. In a 60/40 proposition, you don't clash in the middle and say, 'Now, it's your turn.' Instead, you intersect and overlap, because you're each giving sixty percent."

"Give and it will be given to you." It's the secret in business; it's the secret in interpersonal relationships. And it's the secret of powerful, mountain-moving, miracle-working religion.

Poco's Accident

My daughter Carol was coming home at about ten o'clock one night. We live out in the country, so it is not uncommon to see a dead opossum in the street. As she approached the house, she saw what appeared to be a dead opossum in the reflected headlights. She pulled the car to a stop in the road, got out, realized immediately it was not an opossum. It was our pet dog Poco. Our little Lhasa apso had gotten out, run into the street, and was injured. Carol was shocked when she saw him lying there in the street, apparently dead. But then she heard a whimper and on one foot hopped over to him. Through tears she said, "Poco!" He responded with a painful whimper. Carol tried to lift the weight of the injured dog but she lost her balance and fell. She got back up, but with only one foot she couldn't carry the weight. Just then a car came by and the driver saw this young girl with only one leg trying to lift an injured dog. The driver stopped, jumped out of the car, and said, "May I help you?"

Weeping, Carol said, "Yes, this is my dog. He's been hurt and I know what it's like to get hurt when you've been hit by a car at night. Please help me."

The driver picked up little Poco, who was whimpering, and put him on the front seat. Carol hopped in beside him. *When you care, you really carry.* The good news is that Poco had only a broken jaw and recovered nicely.

You'll Have to Give It Away

Many years ago, my son and I built a little mountain cabin on a remote piece of property up in the mountains in California. It took us a couple of years. We saved our coins and we fixed it up nice and pretty. Finally there was a time when we had it just right. We had a radio in there and a little television set as well. We also had a little place where we could play records and tapes. Our fishing poles were in there and my son had his skis in there. It was well equipped. And then we went up there one weekend to have a nice little rest and we found the door ajar. Then we found a window broken. And we found that all of our property had been stolen. And about that time I got a call from the police department. I was asked to come in and identify the stolen equipment. They thought they'd gotten it all. They asked if I would sign a complaint. They gave me a piece of paper. So I signed, whatever it was. I really don't remember what I signed. Later on I received word that they had caught a couple of men who had ripped us off. I was told they'd been sent to jail. That was it.

I must tell you—I had some bad feelings toward those invisible thieves. Awful feelings. I think it's basically the invasion of your privacy. End of the story? Not quite.

Two, or was it three, years later, I was back in the mountains with my little daughter. We were going through one of the dime stores, buying some balloons for a party. I thought I saw some sinister eyes probing me, from a customer who seemed to be walking up and down the other aisle. And I almost got the feeling that he was following me or staring at me. I went to the cash register and then this character came right up to me. He had on grubby-looking clothes, long hair, and was unshaven. He came real close, with his hands in his pockets, and asked, "Are you Dr. Schuller?" I said, "Yes."

His eyes spoke, he had a smile, tears were in his eyes, his lips trembled. He said, "Will you forgive me?" I said, "Forgive you for what?" He said, "I broke into your home two years ago. I stole your recorder. I stole your television. I stole the skis and the fishing poles." Tears were rolling down his cheeks.

He said, "I went to jail, but that's when it happened." I said, "What?" He said, "I started watching you on television. One of the things I stole from you was a book with your name on it. And somebody's kid was with me. He said, 'You know what? I think this is the Robert Schuller who's on television.' And I said, 'Do you think we ripped him off?' He said, 'Could be.' " Then he said, "I saw you on television and when you asked people to accept Jesus Christ, I did." He continued, "I'm now a Christian. I go to a Bible study here in the mountains, every Wednesday night. Me and a bunch of other kids are born again." He said, "I'm so sorry I did it." And I could tell what he wanted, so I opened my arms and he embraced me. Do you know what? When you really take Christ in your life, you have a connection to the Source of Love that will never let you go. You'll experience salvation and forgiveness of sins. And, you'll never be able to keep it. You'll have to give it away.

Plant a Powerful Seed

I was in Minneapolis recently. I had to speak to about six thousand Methodists. In the forum that followed, one of the ministers asked me this question: "Dr. Schuller, what are you and your congregation doing to fight racism? And what are you doing to fight the social injustices? I never hear you preach any sermons against these sins." I answered him with this story: I was born on an Iowa farm. Every spring my brother and I had to go and pick cockleburs. Cockleburs are ugly, horrible weeds, and every year we had to pull them out, pile them up, and burn them. One spring my father plowed the ground and planted alfalfa. Alfalfa sends roots down twelve feet into the ground. It grew so thick that the cockleburs did not grow—they were choked out.

The positive solution to loneliness, boredom, lust, promiscuity, racism, social injustice, or any sin you can imagine, is not to be against them, but to plant something else so powerful that it consumes the problem. Love is that satisfying! It lifts you beyond temptations. Once you've enjoyed good music, you won't be interested in any other kind. If you are happily married and have a beautiful love in Christ, pornography isn't tempting. Once you've grown alfalfa, cockleburs don't stand a chance. Love is the greatest because it's the answer to every sin you can imagine. Love is the greatest because it's available for all. Love is the greatest because it's the positive solution to every problem.

184

INDEX
OF
NAMES